Ghost Writing

A Step-by-step Guide to Haunt Your Readers

(Launch Your Own Successful Writing Career by Writing Books for Others)

David Bailey

Published By **Regina Loviusher**

David Bailey

All Rights Reserved

Ghost Writing: A Step-by-step Guide to Haunt Your Readers (Launch Your Own Successful Writing Career by Writing Books for Others)

ISBN 978-1-7771462-9-0

No part of this guidebook shall be reproduced in any form without permission in writing from the publisher except in the case of brief quotations embodied in critical articles or reviews.

Legal & Disclaimer

The information contained in this book is not designed to replace or take the place of any form of medicine or professional medical advice. The information in this book has been provided for educational & entertainment purposes only.

The information contained in this book has been compiled from sources deemed reliable, and it is accurate to the best of the Author's knowledge; however, the Author cannot guarantee its accuracy and validity and cannot be held liable for any errors or omissions. Changes are periodically made to this book. You must consult your doctor or get professional medical advice before using any of the suggested remedies, techniques, or information in this book.

Upon using the information contained in this book, you agree to hold harmless the Author from and against any damages, costs, and expenses, including any legal fees potentially resulting from the application of any of the information provided by this guide. This disclaimer applies to any damages or injury caused by the use and application, whether directly or indirectly, of any advice or information presented, whether for breach of contract, tort, negligence, personal injury, criminal intent, or under any other cause of action.

You agree to accept all risks of using the information presented inside this book. You need to consult a professional medical practitioner in order to ensure you are both able and healthy enough to participate in this program.

Table Of Contents

Chapter 1: You would like to become a Writer? 1

Chapter 2: Can You Earn Money Writing? 5

Chapter 3: Free Online Dictionaries 24

Chapter 4: How to Make Cash Writing until Your Book is published............................ 43

Chapter 5: How to determine whether Self-Publishing is the right choice suitable for you 55

Chapter 6: Getting a Novel Published 61

Chapter 7: Tips and Challenges to improve your writing 65

Chapter 8: The job interview.................. 77

Chapter 9: Are you ready to take on any challenge?.. 98

Chapter 10: How to convince people to join... 114

Chapter 11: The Three-Foot-Rule 134

Chapter 12: The unwritten stories of all time 150

Chapter 13: Initial impressions 170

Chapter 1: You would like to become a Writer?

If you're here and you are reading this, then we could imagine that you'd like be a writer and would like to be more informed about the subject. There is no other option but to say that you've landed in the wrong location and it will take time for the information to get into your mind. In any case, you may like to continue reading and you may like the information you read or you could be able to learn something, or at least you might have a good laugh.

Maybe I'm not the right person to give advice on how to become an "good writer", but because I'm an author with a moderate amount of success (under an alternative name) I'm hoping I can offer you a hand.

It is important to practice as is correct spelling and grammar If this phrase made sense for you, then you're in an issue.

The word "practice" is a noun. it is a verb. It is the correct word in this instance. Grammar does not have the spelling "er" and a comma is absent from "important, as". The question of whether "are" should be "is", or whether "are" should be "is" or not remains to be debated by so-called experts However, technically "is" is correct. This is on a 1-table and 4-chair foundation; for example. "There are 4 chairs and 1 table" However "There is 1 table and 4 chairs" in that the verb is supposed to be compatible with the initial item in the list.

"Practice is very important, as is correct spelling and grammar."

The lesson is over however, hopefully you have learned something, (and this version is likely to get through most grammar testers, and will only need to be "grammar" changed). It is not worth writing if you are still required to master the language which is why you first need to learn, then you can write. After that, you should discover a topic that is interesting to you, yet is also interesting for many others. If it is something you're interested in and you are more proficient at writing with more fluid sentences and in a way that is empathetic, but should you wish for readers to take the time to read your work the content needs to be written well and it must be interesting to the readers.

If you've got an article, story or book that you've at least read at least once, and preferably at least twice, to ensure grammar, spelling and other mistakes, what you should accomplish with it is the second issue.

An excellent idea to consider to begin your successful career is to discover a platform where you can publish your piece or short story, to let the general public offer feedback about both the subject as well as your writing abilities. There are numerous sites to test, and each has a lot in common with one. Each one comes with advantages and disadvantages Be sure to read the instructions and the feedback of authors who have already used the website and select the one that is best suitable to your requirements.

Chapter 2: Can You Earn Money Writing?
If you're writing, which is a question to ask if you earn money by writing? The answer is and you could.

But, and this is where the real issue lies most likely not the manner you had envisioned. Be optimistic and don't give the fight, there are methods around this, If you're lucky. This is merely a matter of being able to accept the things you have to take on in order to achieve what you'd like to go. This isn't a way to discourage you instead, it is designed to prepare you for any challenges and provide alternative options as you wait for the answers to come your way.

The dreams of becoming a writer generally involve writing a bestseller sell.

Well, forget it! If you don't have a back-up account that is as big as Bill Gates' or one of the lucky people on earth, just put it aside for the moment.

There are a handful of lucky people who are able to become an acclaimed writer. We are all aware of that. The thing you might not know about this is that

A majority of publishers as well as agents do not take non-solicited manuscripts. They will accept only the work that they have requested. It's an old saying "you won't be able to find work without prior experience, but you cannot gain knowledge because nobody will provide you with work this is true for any work.

If you get a publisher who will take your manuscript and have read your work, here's the next step.

Let's suppose you're an exceptional writer who is bound to be successful, (so about 0.001% of the writing world). Then you write your best-selling book and submit it to magazines, publishers and the list goes on. Today, the average response time for any answer is six to eight months. I've received some replies within a month, and some over two years later. In all that time, you earned zero source of income.

We'll assume that once more, that they are happy with it and sign a contract that you sign only with an expert's guidance. The cost is high and it takes some time. This could take up to one to six months. Trust me when I say you should read the agreement carefully. I've seen clauses like, "Anything written belongs to them and they get a percentage - a large percentage".

Today, I compose the occasional test and logic puzzle since I am enjoying doing it, and also provides me with a little cash to spend. Also, I do translations, for a decent amount however, that meant that the publishers got a share, (40%), in any translation work. This made other tasks practically useless, since I had to settle for too little money, and I needed to request to amend the terms of my contract. After three months, and a lot of emails later, I received an response. The publisher wouldn't alter their decision and it did not work and I needed to start over to find an alternative publisher after having wasted approximately nine months, or one year of waiting.

The second contract I signed said "I confirm the work is all my own and does not infringe on anyone's rights in any way," which was acceptable since it was an entire work of fiction. But, the contract added, "And I accept responsibility if anyone files a claim against the published book for any reason." In the past in the contract it included the words, "The publisher has the right to edit in any way they see fit and to publish and distribute however they wish." If you combine these two elements in a jiffy, that the publisher is able to change names, places and locations to be based on actual people or places and places, however if those actual people file a lawsuit they are my fault.

I was able to try once more to get the contract amended so that it reads, "I accept responsibility for what I wrote, as I wrote it, and only that". After months of debate and messages, they came to an agreement.

I'd say that it probably is a reflection of my luck when it comes to my work. I've won one time, then lose another, however, that's an average between 2 years between getting the work accepted and also lots of time with earning any money.

I also received some contracts under which the publishers would contribute 50% of the funds while I had to pay the remaining. I decided to decline. The reason is that I'd rather pay just a couple of thousand dollars to have my novel published, when I could do it through Amazon or Lulu without cost. The publisher has said that they will publish my book, but If they don't belie in it enough to fund all cost, (a drop in the ocean for them) What would be the results if they promote sales? Additionally, all publishers release books in a traditional manner where they pay all the funds to publish the book. Therefore, they're more likely even if they aren't certain, to promote the book that costs them money, rather than mine that has already been compensated for. This is an attempt to make a compromise, however, it's a half-way to nowhere which is not that is worth spending money on. If you decide to publish your book on your own, and without cost, you should think about what kind of advertising you could accomplish if you spent more than PS3000 on it instead of giving the book to an editor that thinks it's not worthwhile to put their efforts into spending cash on.

In the event that you happen to become J.K. Rowling and make millions from just the same book (unfortunately I've not made even anything like that kind of sum for my novels) although they're exactly the same, of course with a smile) You can go for long time without a source of income.

If you are blessed with an trust fund, a rich husband or other method that provides funds to support your family that's excellent. If not, you must earn your own money for groceries and bills on your own as a writer, there are three main methods that I have found to work.

The other option is joining writing websites There are four websites that can help my needs. Chapter 2: Earning money writing until your book takes off'. I've outlined them, and explained their operation along with their pros and cons, and the things to watch out for.

A different option is to become an author who ghost writes, and in the chaptertitled "All You Need to Know About being a Ghost Writer" I've laid up some suggestions and tips based upon my own experience.

The last thing to consider is creating content for publications, companies as well as private clients, without having to go on websites, and I've discussed my experiences in the section "Writing for Private Clients".

3. Writing tools. Many useful ones, as well as others that are an absolute hindrance

Sometimes, writing may not be the most difficult thing to a writer. It is the other fragments and bits that could cause as much and, in some cases, more than a source of stress. These could include ideas on how to locate free photos to improve the quality of an article or synonyms that can be used instead of a term which may already be used in the text, and numerous other issues. This section is designed to assist authors with this issue by providing free websites for some of these extra challenges.

Grammar Checkers are Usually Wrong

Writers Bane, Automatic Grammar Checkers

It is an accepted reality in the world of English academics that grammar checkers don't perform, but more and more individuals are beginning to consider that they can be a good substitute to human verification.

It is not a secret that they are faster, and they help to reduce time, but what's the purpose of conserving time if your answer isn't correct. You could easily do the calculation that is 132,458,794 multiplied with 67.376 divided by 58999 within 3 seconds, if you do not have the right solution, (151266.02). Just hit the initial button that you see to get the total completed.

It's the same for any grammar checking tool, however my favorite one that I have tested with the greatest frequency is the one used by everyone, Grammerly.

Grammar checkers overlook important mistakes they suggest fixes which are not correct and mark grammatically correct texts as in error - and this is to say that they do not mark "other" English as wrong. A typical American checking tool marks British English as wrong and it is the opposite for Canadian, Irish, Australian, Irish or Canadian English.

One of the issues is the fact that "word usage" can directly alter the character of a sentence however computers don't understand "tone". There are many different methods to express something similar to it, as well as various expressions with multiple interpretations. Again, computers are unable to recognize these variations or inflections.

The simple text until this point - through one of the top grammar checkers yielded the following conclusion: The article has been erroneous and the results are just 51% of the time correct. There are improvements to be made in order to make it more standards.

It is this analysis.

The word that was originally that was in British English "recognised" had to be "recognized" to pass, to be deemed correct, regardless of the fact that I had British English as my language.

Mechanical grammar checkers seem to be having a difficult time distinguishing "between, (for two items), and among, (for more than two)" In this particular article "between English scholars" is considered to be right "as there are not more than two items spoken about in the article", (this is what the article told me) however, between is not correct and reduces my mark, even though "between" isn't correct as is 'among'.

Abbreviations should not be used regardless of the circumstances and there aren't exclusions, as the examiner said. "An American" is wrong since the program states that you should "Use "a" before words that start with consonants" The article that precedes American has to be change. The reason the program believes

American begins with consonants is a mystery to anyone.

"One of the problems" is thought to be too 'wordy' which, in order to be able to get through, there must include "one problem", (even even though it's not an identical issue.). The wording "effect the tone" had to be replaced with "affect the tone", but interestingly, after it was modified the program stated that the sentence was not correct and was then necessary to change it back and then, the program said it was incorrect and again.

It could leave you even with more confusion than you were before you even started, because often there is any way to attain 100 percentage. Whatever word you select, it is likely to be incorrect, and often choosing the wrong term could result in an increased percentage so you'll be able to pass.

Computer programming languages have specific grammar and syntax that isn't natural language.

Passive voice which is regarded as formal, is frequently censored by computers, and the active voice is marked as the right voice.

It certainly promotes poor grammar and promotes exceptionally poor writing, and must be prohibited.

Linguists as well as English professors are of the same opinion that grammar checks are typically incorrect to the point that they "do more harm than good" and "for the most part, accepting the advice of a computer grammar checker on your prose will make it much worse, sometimes hilariously incoherent".

The person who invented the machines that "do the job of a human in one hundredth of the time, and just as well" can't have had any knowledge of grammar or writing.

First of all, English that is the primary language used on the World Wide Web, comes in a variety of versions - each of which are deemed to be acceptable by their countries.

Since the creators of this "time saving wonders" seem to be predominantly American and it's that the language they use that is "correct", while anything else is, at least otherwise, deemed "wrong".

If someone wanted to make a point, "English" is from England and, therefore, is usually referred to in the UK as "The Queen's English", therefore anything else that is not English is untrue.

Human beings are having a broad mind, and so acceptance of the English that is spoken to be spoken in America, Canada, Ireland, Australia, South Africa as well as all other countries in which English is their official spoken language is the norm.

The art of writing isn't just focused on correct grammar since there are times when "incorrect grammar" is actually right. This conveys the meaning of the simplest form "He said as what he don't like it," immediately letting readers know that this is a non-cultured individual It could be an elegant method to communicate this message rather than a straightforward "he's a complete beginner at write and read' to define the person speaking.

If you have a conversation with one who states, "Me thinks he doeth protest too much", it's not correct to write in the first place. When I talked to him, he stated that "I believe he is protesting too much" however that is the only thing needed for passing the grammar checker that is mechanical.

You can use the phrase, "While on holiday in Italy I heard someone say "vuoi gelato?", and I assumed they were asking if I was cold, when they were actually enquiring if I wanted an ice-cream" It will lead to a certain errors in grammar. This is also the case with the instruction "run on sentences and incomplete phrase - you forgot the beginning".

Well-structured sentences that are passive are not a good idea, since they appear wrong to computers, therefore it's best to write like an imbecile of five years old, who's first language isn't English. They are a sure way to pass grammar-checkers (Grammarly being the primary reason).

They also seem to be incapable or not programmed to differentiate between fiction and fact. There are numerous articles that are on the web, and scanned by these checkers, which declare that "migraine is a headache". The statement is false, accurate and misleading. It is a neurologic disorder that is sometimes referred to as an illness that is debilitating. The only thing it's not is headache. One characteristic symptom associated with this disease is headache. Therefore, a computer hearing the term "headache" associated with migraine thinks this is true. The machine does not evaluate the location or frequency of the term.

The notion of being "free" to write is no longer a thing in the past if we allow it to be. There is a need for purchasing programs to make sure you are in compliance with different programs to ensure the majority of your work as you can is "American" in structure.

Use these tools only for your own personal use make use of your knowledge of the language and sure, it's fine to test a story on an automated system to verify your work. However, only take corrections that you're confident are accurate.

Grammar checkers have caused a sadness lower of writing standards in general.

Free Resources for Writers, Dictionaries

Chapter 3: Free Online Dictionaries

The first thing to consider is that a dictionary is essential, since it is not just helpful in the area of vocabulary, but also particular theme-related terms, their origins the words, and words that are similar to each other. Many writers use a dictionary and don't need for a second one. Likewise, it is included in the majority of word processing programs however, they tend to have a basic structure.

There are many benefits to having an online dictionary

* Price - only if it's not

* It does not take up any area on any computer, and since it's online

* It's updated than the version you purchase (most dictionary do not offer updates unless you purchase a updated version).

The best free dictionary you can make use of online is "The Free Dictionary",

The homepage page is packed with related and unrelated objects, but do not feel discouraged - the page can be modified quickly and efficiently and your preferences are saved and are retained for future sessions.

This online dictionary is available and you can save it as a bookmark or save it to your toolbars for easy usage.

When you type in an expression, not just is the meaning displayed but there are a number of other options including learning more about it through a relevant hyperlink, (usually Wikipedia - not the most reliable resource) or making the word appear in many different languages. Answers to the questions provide multiple definitions, and also tell you which other dictionary definitions contain the word (medical or legal. See below for a comprehensive listing). This will tell you the history of the word. You are able to listen to the pronunciation (in both American as well as British English), synonyms and related terms, as well as antonyms and much more.

The sources included in this dictionary are:

* dictionary

* Thesaurus

* medical dictionary

* legal dictionary

* financial dictionary

*idioms

* Abbreviations

*encyclopedia

* A translation of the word

* Many different languages

Word games to increase vocabulary

* a lot more

It's a great tiny tool. Although I've got an Oxford English Dictionary installed on my personal computer (I am British at heart) I utilize this online dictionary to search for technical terms, languages, as well as other options.

One great website to check for signs for symptoms is The Thesaurus.com. It provides a variety of instances, synonyms, as well as related terms. You can easily change the vocabulary you use.

Checking for errors

Word is able to do an excellent job in identifying errors, but it's not able to catch them all. In addition, it identifies some things as errors, but they're true.

Paperrater is a no-cost platform to check the quality of your writing. The trial version can only let you upload approximately 3-4 pages in one time. If you're working on an entire book, it can be a lengthy process, however it's the most efficient I've found. I've tried a variety of.

Free Plagiarism Checkers

At first, this might not be something that you believe is necessary, but in reality it's a valuable source. There is so much published on so many topics it's easy to write a piece in the same manner as another individual without consciously doing so however, if you decide to release it, you might get in trouble by copying or plagiarising works.

There are numerous programs to determine if an item or work of art is genuine Some websites claim that they run your work through a specific program for verification, meaning you could lose any good standing in the event that the "original article" is found as being too identical to an already-existing piece.

I've tested a number of them and have found that none are is 100% reliable, including the most expensive and well-known one. I typically use four different gratis ones, and if provide the same results I'll hope for the best.

plagiarisma.net

This Free Plagiarism Checker on this website is only able to be used for a certain amount of usage before asking for your permission to join. It is free to join and they don't deliver junk or spam mail. Therefore, there's no reason to not sign up. I've joined for a long period of time and never received a single unwanted email.

The free membership gives you only a few searches each day. However, this is enough for many writer's needs. It is possible to upgrade your membership at a cost of a modest amount - or, if you publish a review or article about them, and they are happy with the piece or review, you can get an upgrade for free.

The program can be used either online or downloaded (Windows).

Plagiarismnet is one step more than the other tools and gives an alternative to check for similarities, and the results show the percent that indicates "sameness".

A further feature of this program over the other software is the fact that multiple languages are available.

Results vary, but they give around 60% precision.

searchenginereports.net

The results are not high in my top ten list because the data is generally not as precise as others. However, sometimes through a lucky chance the results can provide details that others missed.

When it is successful when it does, it's the most effective however, this happens only about 60 percent of the times. It has offered me "original content" for work that I've already published and if the title says "original", do not trust it. Try another version, however when it states, "copied", believe that it is true.

The document explains exactly where the original piece can be found, going beyond saying that other copies exist dating prior to this one and which ones are. It is possible to select the degree in "sameness", but the greater the degree, the more slowly the outcomes will be coming and so take your time.

duplichecker.com

This too is a bit hit and miss, and like searchenginereports.net shows detail when found, but more often than not it does not find anything, even when you know it is there because you published it yourself! Once a copy has been found, this program shows the location of the file is.

It accepts both text and files, but it does say .txt documents I've used different extensions and have had success.

It's about 25-30% accurate.

dustball.com

It's good, nothing more, not less. When it's checked the documents, the document, a "possible plagiarism" button appears when you click it. will show you the exact location where the document is. It's an example of a Google webpage, however those relevant sections are highlighted to make it easier for using.

It is approximately 50percent exact.

For all these programs, "no copies found" does not mean that it is true, however "plagiarism detected" is.

Free, Legal Images

Covers are required for your novel if you're planning to self-publish. And many publishers require the finished book, therefore they also require it.

Royalty Free Images are usually typically not available for download. This is simply an advertising strategy that entices the viewer and they are looking for money they can call under a different name. However, it is as Shakespeare could have put it, "A Royalty by any different name ..".

If you decide to use images that are not owned by you, or from any other source on the web, make sure you be sure to read the rules and comply with the "rights" related guidelines. If you are using images that are free, this typically requires attribution, and sometimes an acknowledgement to the artist. The site you visit will inform you the conditions to be met.

Here is a list of websites that provide legally-free, free images that any writer, or any other person could make use of.

Pexels provide top-quality photos with a variety of freebies and some that require the attribution. I usually give credit regardless of whether I am asked since someone developed this project and deserves to be recognized. There's an enormous selection of high-quality photos from various subjects.

Wikimedia Commons is home to a wide variety of images, symbols as well as designs, and it appears to be solely attribution. It's a vast collection and almost too large that the chances of reworking a lookup are virtually zero. That means you have to search through an abundance of low-quality images in order to locate the best one for the purpose you are looking for. If you persist, there's an excellent chance that you'll discover what you are seeking, however there is a reason why many, or all of the photos aren't nearly the same quality as those on other websites. There are times when the picture isn't great. and may be blemished with a background, or other items that are not connected to the object you're trying to display.

This is a great option for historical images or places that are obscure that are, basically, items you can't find elsewhere.

Flickr is a crowdsourced site so you will never have a clue what you might come across. Users take photos of the oddest things, and some even upload pictures that appear out of focus However, the selection is vast and worthy of a look in the event that you can't locate the photo on other sites. Also, this is attribution required and usually a hyperlink back to the original owner is required.

Morgue File and Stock Exchange are excellent websites and very similar in a number of ways. Images that are on Morgue Files have a better appearance, and you don't have to inquire about what I am talking about since it's more of a perception that they are superior photos. However, both sites offer an excellent selection and search using keyword, category or. On Morgue images, but it is not possible to search for Stock Exchange. Stock Exchange.

Certain images that are available on Stock Exchange are not free You'll must scrutinize the images you've decided to apply. The majority of them are listed with the tag "premium results" and are displayed in a vertical band on the top. If you expand, there will be costs.

Both sites also work with "image credit", so make sure to use them.

The most popular site to get photos can be found on Every Stock Photo, but it's not as simple what they seem. This site examines other websites (about 12 in total, not including those previously mentioned) to find the exact photo you're looking for and the result is amazing.

Two main issues that I have observed. The first is that the data comes about 80% of Flickr as well as users on this site often give names that are only relevant to them. Stonehenge is a name that says "A Horseshoe", for example. If you're searching for Stonehenge the image will not be displayed, and in the case of the horseshoe it's Stonehenge.

Another issue is that each website has their individual image rights rules and conditions. You should read through them all prior to deciding on which image is suitable or can be used in a way.

It allows you to sort results by license or source (you are able to remove Flickr) sizes, etc. therefore you are able to choose which websites you want to search.

What is interesting concerning these tools is that a lot of them are superior to their more expensive competitors. They have no cost because certain brands have dominated the market and left no room for any other cost-based programs. It's a shame because the majority of them are excellent.

N.B. Beware about Google images. There are many images that appear placed there with no permission from the owner. One of my photos was uploaded to trip advisor that Google has put up in Google Images without my permission and I needed to issue an additional DMCA Takedown notice to get the photo removed.

Language Translators

A machine-driven translator could be a useful tool if it is it is used as a personal interest or for a hobby however, it is not an essential tool for business.

There are times when you come across information in a different language and would like to find out what the information says to incorporate, or not include to include in the piece that you write, however most translators don't have the best information. When they spew forth complete rubbish, this is not sensible however if they provide you with something that looks reasonable data, then you might think it is accurate. It is often contrary to what was originally stated.

Two translators can be used for the majority of personal uses. I've tried a variety of devices. I've only tried basic French as well as Spanish as well as Italian but I am unable to testify for other languages (even my French isn't perfect) However, they function effectively enough to give you some idea of what the article is about.

Frengly and Lookwayup

The two platforms support multiple languages and offer decent translations most times. However, they only work with small bits of text. A brief paragraph is the minimum it can be at any one moment.

I work as a translator I am currently unemployed as businesses aren't able to see any reason to give me a lot of dollars when machines can complete the job for free.

"Our business confirms that we are always at the lead, displaying the latest range of goods approved by Rina. We were involved in the complete process of the Italian nautical industry since 1926, playing the leading role throughout all stages of marketing that is constantly changing. Our company was the first to be homologated in 1995."

One firm that rejected my request to translate Italian to English in their name, has released this.

The correct wording should be "Our company is at the leading position in the world of cosmetics. Our products are thoroughly checked and certified prior to going into the market. Our exports have been going out and have had great success since 1926. The first cosmetics business to adopt a green policy in the year 1995.

Naturally, that's quite a bit of nonsense that isn't true however, it's acceptable..

Because these folks don't have a basic understanding of English They believe it as accurate and straightforward and, more important the fact that it's absolutely free. Even if it doesn't result in the creation of new businesses cannot be considered a reason to not use it.

However, if you're looking to add the phrase in another language, or to verify an item that is not English Try two websites for a guarantee of the accuracy.

Chapter 4: How to Make Cash Writing until Your Book is published

Below are some websites where you can make money by writing, while you wait for that big break.

Each writing website I've used (and I believe I've used each one) I have found them to be almost identical however they're not perfect.

Everyone says they get the amount of a portion, which is usually 20%. However, there are some odd tax rates and expenses can also be taken from the share you earn, making the earnings you earn 75% not 80%..

These sites seem to disregard the fact that without writers they'd be unable to jobs. They make their money primarily through clients and they go to great lengths to make sure they are happy even throwing writers down for doing so. After you've earned your cash, it may last up to three weeks before receiving it. This is longer than what the company claims to give you.

They're not properly set up or efficient. None of them work despite the fact that it's easy to make couple of changes to make the system running more smoothly, faster and bring greater ROI.

The main issue is the competition from writers who "blow their trumpets higher than you' and are willing to do so for pennies.

I've seen ads for jobs "Book Wanted - 30-35,000 Words with a payment of $20' and the job had 53 options to apply!

A different job required the delivery of 500,000 words in three weeks. A bidder paid $20 to complete the task in just three days.

There is no way to beat that So don't attempt. If the customer wants to spend $20 or has a large volume that is written faster than it's physically feasible and they don't care in the quality of writing, they just want speedy and inexpensive.

It is a real account of a journalist who receives 98% of reviews over 87 job openings, (believe it or not). They are rated by the site as the highest of its employees. It is a serious error in the way a site has been designed to declare this individual as "one of our most prestigious members'.

I'm XXXXXXX. full time, fast and effective writer. I am the perfect person for writing me based assignment.

This time, I'm looking forward to exploring my interests in the past and write.

Writing is an inborn characteristic of me and I'd like to be successful in this field.

I'm quick to type and I have an excellent knowledge of English. My content is exclusive, free of errors, and plagiarism-free and thoroughly researched. I make sure to provide my work quickly and flawlessly.

My aim is to provide my customers with top performance and quality in my writings.

I'm an extremely versatile person in my vocabulary, and have excellent spelling and grammar. I'm quick and efficient and can complete task in a speedy trip.

I'm the one who can do urgent work quickly!

Do not hesitate to request it if the person is needed.

In my time as an English teacher, I could have given this a mark of 10%, but that was is only due to the fact that they completed their work. What is the best way to correct the problem... in essence, it isn't something that I'd correct since it's all being re-written.

There's another issue: the need for good feedback in order to be hired, however it isn't possible to get a job until you've received feedback. This is the solution finding a job that pays a little yet simple task "300 words blog for eight dollars'. If the blog's title is what you want to promote your blog's content is, then write it in the proposal, and then offer it at $5. If you receive a couple of them, and get good comments, you're now in the right place to get started.

There are jobs on every site and you submit your application. You choose a writer place the funds in escrow and then you finish the work, and it gets confirmed and then the funds are transferred to the writer.

Here are the 4 websites I have used and on which I earn money, though it's not always huge.

You can count on 25% of the money going to your site at some point or other. When clients pay and released the funds quickly and when you ask for the payment, it happens quickly in a matter of 1-2 days typically. The last time I checked, it was 21 days (due to Covid that they claimed to have, but I am unable to comprehend why Covid causes the company to wait up to 21 days to hit the button for releasing the funds.)

In the event of any issues like clients not showing up, (which happens more often than you might think) then they will take the money from the escrow within 7 days.

When a customer complains that they don't want to make a payment because they believe the work has not been adequate, PPH tend to take the side of the client. There was a customer who with 10 articles who did this (and I later discovered that she'd posted all of them on her site) And PPH let her down and refused to pay. I wrote to complain, noting the work was used in a way that was illegal, and without paying for 3 months, and three months later and a lot of emails, they concluded they were right. Then I made an DMCA removal note to her website hosts. (Stolen or plagiarized content can be taken off a site upon request by the person who owns the copyright. It could also be shut down.) Her website was shut and down in a matter of minutes. I was required to shell out PS9 to submit an official complaint to PPH that I was able to get back as I won, however, this is a joke and is just one of many instances where the customer prefers the worker over the client.

The most lucrative jobs are usually found posted on this website, however mostly for blogs and articles, and so on, not for books.

There are many very well pay jobs. There are also extremely low-paying but fast ones. (write two quiz questions at $15).

You receive a specific number of proposals for every month for free and you can purchase additional. I don't pay additional items, but I do make sure to choose carefully the bids I place on.

The quality of the client service and employees is what I have found superior to other websites. The site also serves different areas, including design and photographers, accountants, accountants, etc.

Again fees etc. consume around 25% of what you receive. The money is 'in pending' as long as one month. It could take several days, or even longer to receive the money. In general, I count three weeks until I am able to have access to my income.

There are more job opportunities this site than on other websites However, clients can not be clear enough. For instance, they might say 'need writer to write 4 blogs per week and they do not define what the topic is. In PPH there is the option to ask "clarification queries', however on Upwork it is required to pay for that.

Additionally, you get a specific quantity of bids or connects, or 'connects' as they are referred to each month.

Customers leave feedback two times, one feedback is made public, the other remains private.

The first four jobs I did received a public rating of five stars, which is 100 percent.

Every client requested additional work. So they must have been pleased with the job. After my private feedback was made public, (yes, it isn't quite as private as it could be. In fact, it's merely private) the number of clients I had decreased to 72 percent. A client of mine gave me a five-star feedback in all areas, (there are a few areas to consider: delivery times; precision, skills etc.) I called the website and pointed out that one piece of comments was clearly not true, however I the site claimed that it was their opinion which they were entitled to an right to it. They would not accept the fact that a customer who truly considered my work to be terrible would not have demanded additional feedback. They did not acknowledge that the'secret' feedback shouldn't not be displayed in my profile, or even that by requesting two kinds of votes the people they urged to fake. However, the bad marks persisted and I was unable to gain work in order to improve my score. (I did manage it.)

There are many opportunities to write books for ghostwriting that are both non and fiction on this website in addition to writing articles. However, the pay rate is usually low.

Freelancer (https://www.freelancer.com)

A lot of jobs pay very little and some are extremely low and you can find a lot of offers for them. But, the good news is that you can are offered free bids monthly which means that trying is free. There have been people who accepted my bid which was best by far. This was because they believed my work was worthwhile.

I have a hard time getting jobs here, mostly because they have a very low pay rate and I'm reluctant to make a bid. However, this site pays 10% much less than other websites.

There's plenty articles writing opportunities in the area however, there aren't many books.

The payment takes about a week (small cost to transfer cash, typically $0.99)

As with other sites, there are monthly bids for free So, trying it for free.

The pay is low however, the amount of time required to complete it usually is shorter. If you're fast it is possible to fit 10,000 words as you search for higher-paying job.

There are various other sites for writing also, but after when I tried them and found them to be ineffective. But that doesn't mean that they cannot be useful, however, so take a look and see what you can find. Be wary of those who provide payment per click to your work.

Chapter 5: How to determine whether Self-Publishing is the right choice suitable for you

The book you wrote is finished you want to put the publication in print, but there are many options and you don't know how to begin. Next, you must consider the pros and cons of conventional publishing, self-publishing or printing-on-demand, or e-book publishing.

This article examines the advantages and disadvantages of self-publishing.

* Pros

The publisher is you and, as such, have the complete influence over the way the book is made. Which graphics are employed and how the book is laid out as well as what the jacket and title will be, and so on.

* There aren't agents, editors or publishers who all take a percentage from your profits.

Nobody can force how to take away a part which could be the best portion of the story.

* You decide the cost of the book as well as any discounts or sales.

All rights in the book will remain in your control.

* You are able to publish work which publishing houses don't wish to take on. It could be a novel about a specific subject, or a poem, since these aren't the best-selling books and don't bring in enough revenue for many publishing houses to take an interest.

It will go to the public much faster when published by an agency for publishing.

* If you're able to have an already-created reading audience (for example or someone who's an knowledgeable in a particular field and also gives talks, you

can make the book available at such events) it gives you greater flexibility to write, and also greater profit from selling the book.

* Cons

* You must make a payment to purchase the print copies of your book, unless, of course, you create an eBook to offer for sale.

All the earnings are yours for the taking, as are all costs (perhaps the cost of hiring an artist design the cover) So this could create a challenge to earn any profits.

It is essential to promote your book on your own, otherwise person will be aware of it and what it's about, or the best place to purchase the book.

If you're just looking for the satisfaction of putting your work published in book format Consider other options like print-on demand, for instance handful of copies are enough. This kind of publishing, which is known, only creates sales for families and friends who believe they are required to purchase the work.

* Not just a huge amount of money required for self-publishing it also requires a significant amount of time spent editing the format, formatting and other aspects which means you may not be able to create another book, or even a sequel.

Self-published titles are considered by many as "not published" by the publishing world. The challenge is for if not impossible to find an individual who will review your book. Shops will hesitate to sell books, and libraries don't require one title when you can get multiple publications from major publishers.

It is essential to edit and proofread your work carefully and it is typically more straightforward for projects that are non-yours because you know exactly the words you intended to use and are able to comprehend the meaning however others might not be able to understand.

* You will need to get a the ISBN number of your book to ensure the chance to succeed, which can cost you.

You will need to prepare the book as well as graphic designs from the source.

It is important to keep the books in storage after they've been printed and delivered is up to you, but it may require more space than you imagine, and many self-publishers compel users to keep a specific number.

Marketing must be handled by the person who is doing it.

* The advertising is entirely up to you.

However, even if you do manage to make revenue, you must receive orders and then deliver your books.

You could require a license for self-publishing from your business and publish, so make sure you ask the authorities of your country.

The cons surpass the advantages, and you must be certain you've made the right decision for your project and that you will need a substantial amount of funds as well as time and resource. Self-publishing has been very successful for some people, but it is in a majority.

Chapter 6: Getting a Novel Published

Publishing a novel is harder than getting gold. Most publishers won't accept unpublished manuscripts. This requires that you know about them before they even consider reading the work.

Smaller independent publishers are typically an ideal way to get started since they don't have rigid methods. Look for one that is publishing your genre of writing. Literary agencies are another option as they can connect with editors on your behalf, however they require a portion of the money you make and, often, this agreement can last for several books when you're successful. Take the time to study it and not agree to any conditions you're not comfortable with. Request that they be removed or changed. It is possible to do this.

If you have found a publisher that is suitable and read their guidelines, you must go through the author's guideline for each publisher. Because should you provide material they do not like the request could be rejected immediately. In this phase, some publishers want only a summary, while others require only the first page and others want the complete book.

Create a cover letter that's short and clear. It should include the person you are and your previous experience (be truthful, as they will be able to examine and if they find the discrepancies they could be able to blacklist you) Then, review the text. The summary should be just 2 or 3 paragraphs since all publishers are receiving a plethora of daily new titles and frequently feel uneasy reading lengthy letters.

Make sure to send it to one of your preferred publisher and then wait up to four weeks. There are some publishers who provide timelines to respond, so you should wait for the right time then send an mail asking them if they've received your submission and when you should expect to hear from them.

If you're rejected for your project, Don't give up. Certain companies will tell you the reason why they're not interested, and you must review your writing, looking at their comments to determine if changes can assist. If there is no explanation, you can continue to send your manuscript to various publishing houses until you have enough rejections that let you know that the piece isn't satisfactory enough or you get you receive an acceptance.

My story was repeatedly rejected before I was able to sell the story to a customer. The story was then published through Amazon with the client's permission and was able to make it to the top 5 of the category.

If you are accepted for publication, then you'll probably have seek out a legal opinion regarding the contract to ensure that you're not signing a document which only benefits of the publisher and provides nothing to gain for you.

Be aware the fact that an advance can be just an advance, which is then taken out of your profits at a later date. The amount of advance can indicate how many the publisher is expecting to sell. For instance, they may provide you with $55,000 if they are convinced that they will sell 100 copies However, the fact that they offer you a $10 advance doesn't necessarily mean that they think sales will be minimal. The main benefit of the large amount of advance is when you are in need of money quickly which makes publishers more eager to increase sales since they are trying in order to recover this amount.

Chapter 7: Tips and Challenges to improve your writing

I'm a English instructor and an author who has been published.

I'll set you some tasks to improve your writing (hopefully). Each challenge 1,2,4 5, 6 and 1 are created to assist with a specific aspect of writing: narrative, description timeline, characters and tone of voice.

It isn't a class, this is just a couple of exercises designed to improve the writing process.

1. Create a 500-word story. Then write it using 150/100 words. Do the 300-400 words that you omitted essential? Are they adding anything to the narrative? If not, take them out.

2. Pick a location or area, create a brief description. Then, the reader will be able to see the area, the beach, or clearing etc.

3. Make an obstacle to your tale and overcome it

4. In less than 1000 words, write about two main characters. Let readers feel a connection with one, and fear or hate one. This is not a list of characteristics or a description of them. The information can be split into parts of a book. One person writing about a character in one portion then another person doing the same in the next or all be a single piece.

5. Create a short story and sketch it out on an outline of a timeline. Beginning the line on the date you first wrote in the story, and then draw with the paper still on until the tale is finished. Does the line appear messy difficult to follow? Or is it clean and simple to follow? The line doesn't have to be straight but it should be clear enough to follow when there are a lot of turns)

6. Write a 500-word story that is written from a Zebra's perspective. Zebras can communicate with other species or even humans.

It's not as bad as it appears. Writing can be essential to write in a different perspective, and with a different tone. The zebra's name is an exaggeration.

7. Make sure you write an opening paragraph that entices readers to continue reading.

8. Create a conclusion paragraph that makes the reader want to read more of your tales.

9. Create a short outline of the elements of the story that are required in order to run smoothly and who the protagonist is what, when and why; a an authentic plot, etc.

10. Create a dialogue with persons that is minimum 20 words, (not with the same person).

11. Rewrite the sentences, removing repetitive words and replace the words with new ones, while making the message the same.

12. Make an atmosphere. For example, My garden was in full bloom and I could hear him talking through the wall behind him.

OR

There was a high wooden wall which separated the garden of my house and that of his while I was standing on the wall, I was able to hear a voice say something. The voice came through the wall. Being unable to see the man made it sound like a spooky.

13. Be sure not to delay the final check/change. It's easy to go through good

work and then work over it to the point that the flow is not as good as it should. Take a break as soon as you think it's good. Return a couple of days after and then check.

14. Do check your facts. If you record that it became darkness during the day in New York at five in the afternoon, make sure it is actually when the it gets dark. I read about an author with a huge following who wrote 'Buon Nuit rather than "bonne nuit," but they didn't not mean goodnight. They signified "good evening".

15. Do not confuse mystery and obscurity.

Do not fall into the false impression that because something is hard to comprehend is a reason to provide a sense of mystery and draw the attention of readers. That is not always the case. Be sure to not compromise clarity for intelligence. The majority of people do not like being able to comprehend things that are confusing no matter if this result is deliberate or by accident. Do not be enticed to become complex just for the sake of complexity.

Tips

I write down my protagonist's names, jobs etc. and then put it in the conclusion of my story I am writing. This is what I could see fast 'David is married Jennifer. He's an accountant.'

After reading a couple of books it is common for characters to move around a little; this allows you to identify who an individual is.

My writing is never checked until I'm done. It can interrupt the flow but it's only for me. I have friends who are checking while they write Find out what is most effectively for you.

Ghost Writing and Tips, tricks and even stories

Make clear the steps ahead and be sure to ask as many questions that you'll need before starting for example. Do you have names that you'd like? Are there any names you'd rather not have?

A lot of people want to write 25 pages, which claims to contain 10,000 words but in reality the truth is that it's not. It is 7,000 - 8,000. Find out what they are looking for. If the request is for 25 pages, then you've saved the equivalent of 2,000 words and make more.

Be sure to point at obvious issues. There was a customer who desired John, James, Johnny and Jack. I told him that I believed the readers might struggle to figure out what they were, since the names are too similar which is why we chose Philip, James, Michael and Will.

Make it clear that anyone who claims they can compose 500,000 words at $20 in three days likely to be lying (unless they have already done) The odds that they're not worth the cost, are extremely high. And yes, this exact quote was presented.

If the genre is romance Ask which genre? What do they mean by "steamy"?

Although I'm not sure, and don't know what my customers are but I am able to say that they are a few ignorant of the books. There was a customer who requested an Regency Romance. I am a huge fan of these books, and I was thrilled, however it was a bit expensive for any book, and especially the one I chose. I made the point that there was a lot of reviewing of the terms including 'vouchers to Almacks and Almacks', but I wasn't certain of the spelling, necktie terminology, etc so, and would prefer to be paid more than what she was charging.

The lady didn't know what I was talking about and simply said "I just need to add the date for it to be regency. You can create a contemporary romance and state that it's 1840 in the beginning'.

A majority of my clients are unaware the meaning of a draft and they make comments such as"Serrret is spelled incorrectly on page 15, there's no Monday on it; John is not David's brother, and the word 'commitment' is spelling incorrectly...

I will always inform them in the beginning that I'll provide an initial draft that will be flawed, but I'll correct them in the final draft. However, they will still highlight numerous mistakes.

You must ensure that the client is satisfied. It's worth the effort to ensure this happens because negative feedback is a nightmare to recover.

Get money into escrow before you start. Don't work without funds being available. I came up with an unintentional 177-page document that I could not find reason to use because the client were not paying, (they did not see the piece, so it was not a matter of the quality; they simply disappeared. In fact, as a trusting person in my nature, it did take me this long to work out the issue.)

Check out contracts carefully - they often state that you didn't duplicate and that you're responsible when it's discovered that you copied it, (fair enough), however, they often state that the client is free to alter it however they wish - and that's reasonable. Problems arise where the contract states that you did not copy, and you are accountable once it's published, in the event that it turns out you copied'. When you sign it to the customer, they can fill whatever they like or even plagiarized some thing. Make sure they change it so that it reads 'you didn't take a copy, and you're responsible for your work in the event that it turns out you have copied. Keep a copy. (I own one USB filled with the entire publications I wrote on it.

Make sure to set a more extended time frame for delivery than is necessary. There is no way to know what will happen if a problem arises. A tooth that is broken could delay your work by for a whole day. If the deadline is short, it may cause you to miss. The client could not pay or ask for the entire amount or lesser. Again, it can mean negative feedback.

Keep in mind the costs. The site often charge 20%. It will end up to be 25%, as they include taxes. Or so they claim. Transfers to banks or other financial institutions are expensive, and could cost more the money you receive (like with

PayPal). That $100 that you believed you'd earn in a short time turns into 70 dollars.

Chapter 8: The job interview

A brief overview of one minute

In this chapter

The description of the job

The very first ghostwriters

What is a ghostwriter to do? What are the reasons why ghostwriters are necessary? for the job the interview

• The abilities a ghostwriter requires # The thrill factor

A profile of a great ghostwriter your bow

The description of the job

What exactly is the definition of a ghostwriter? The majority of writers understand"ghostwriter" as a term. A lot of readers do not. After I shared with one person about my newest project writing a ghost story to someone else, they got very excited and informed me that they enjoyed ghost stories. Ghostwriting does not have anything related to sitting in graveyards or haunted homes for hours on end and recording what you might have observed, or even hoped you'd witnessed. No old warriors with their heads draped under their arms. No rattling chains. Exorcisms and hauntings are not permitted.

Note down - ask several of your friends who are not writers whether they are aware of what a ghostwriter actually is and what they do.

Writers are considered ghosts as they're the unnoticed source of the work presented. Write something for someone else and you get recognition. The name of the client appears included in the book, story, the article or the blog. Your client is the one who gets all the press. It may be permitted to stand in line and be invisible when signings are taking place, but you might not. Certain clients will not allow it.

Your client arranges the interviews for publications, magazines as well as radio and television. You may have been asked for assistance before making the interview. "What should I say when I am asked what I think about this or something else? The work you do may not end until the release of the book. Ghosts can be required for advice or even the moral support needed by the client, however you'll be in the background. In your role as their ghost, you'll write the piece, then take the cash and remain quiet. There's nothing scary about it!

Ghostwriters provides a professional service that includes writing the task and let the client to get the credits. In order to do this, you must to be passionate about creating for your own enjoyment and not become someone who writes just to make a name for themselves.

The ghostwriters who were the first to be hired.

It has been a profession perhaps since the beginning of writing.

There's a conspiracy theory about the author of Shakespeare's plays. Can a country boy Will actually have composed them himself? Wouldn't Stratford somewhat out of the norm of life in the day? Who could be aware of such specifics about the locations he wrote about? A variety of names have been proposed as possible writers. Potential candidates include those with a high level of travel and educated such as Edward de Vere, Ben Jonson, Christopher Marlowe or the Earl of Oxford. Maybe William did write the plays by himself, with no ghost to be found.

Auguste Jules Maquet was a ghostwriter. He seemed to be content with his job initially, but following a dispute over finances, he ended up being in the courtroom together with his partner in writing. This is a hint at the person Auguste ghosted. In the graveyard of Paris"Pere-Lachaise", the name inscribed on his gravestone read "The Three Musketeers, The Count of Monte Cristo and La Reine Margot. It has been suggested theorize that Monsieur Maquet was responsible for the original text for The Three Musketeers but he could not get the text published because the author was not his name. The story is the same! This is when Alexander Dumas stepped in. Dumas was a renowned author, yet he was with financial trouble. The work of Maquet was, allegedly it was published under Dumas's name which is how a lucrative partnership started. Both authors, but as Dumas got the credit, Maquet remained the ghost.

The two examples mentioned-- Shakespeare and Dumaswere controversially debated. Are their works ghostwritten? Are they the same men who were mentioned actually create their own works? Perhaps we won't be able to say for certain.

For a while in the past, ghosting was not a thing. A majority of people thought that all books were created with the name of whoever was in the book's cover. Wrong! What kind of person who lives the life of a busy, hectic person with a lot of obligations take the enough time to write their personal tale? It's likely that they did not. They hired ghostwriters to help their company. Then, in the last few years, some ghosts have stepped into the spotlight. A few ghosted authors admit that they received help in creating their books.

A lot of us have been aware of Andrew Crofts. He is a well-known ghostwriter. What's that? Well-known ghostwriter? This is the reason behind his writing career which Andrew Crofts has become a well-known name. He has written Sold for Zhana Musen, who aged 15 she was sold to her father to become the child bride. Andrew Crofts has ghosted many autobiographies of famous people, including Jimmy Nail, Pete Bennett winner of BBC's Big Brother series, Melissa Bell who is the mother of XF's Alexandra Burke, Bette Davies Gillian Taylforth, Bette Davies ... The list is endless. Each of John Prescott and Paul Gascoigne were able to have their stories written by Hunter Davies. Katie Price (a.k.a. Jordan, the model Jordan) was the author of several novellas and autobiographies. The ghost of her of the model Jordan was Rebecca Farnworth.

A lot of people are unaware that celebrity lives are not composed by the people who appear on the front cover of the book or in fact, that the novels composed by stars are typically composed by a name that isn't known to the author.

It's only since the last few years that ghosts have emerged from the shadows and have demanded attention. A few have come out to get some spotlight but many remain a secret and others have contracts to protect their secret. Do you want to join the ranks of these criminals even if it's just taking a dip? Continue reading and discover what you need to know.

What is a ghostwriter's job?

Ghostwriting doesn't have to be restricted to the controversial or glamorous personal stories of famous people. Ghostwriters can write whatever the client would like they write. These could be speech, resumes, letters or articles, stories or life-stories, individual stories, blogs, adverts poetry, and an array of other stuff.

Ghostwriters have their own websites to be easily reached if someone would like to work with them. They also find jobs for themselves, by promoting their services, and searching online possibilities. Thanks to the advent of the internet, openings for ghostwriters are expanding every day, but they must be vetted carefully. Be wary of committing to a large amount of work in exchange for the sake of a non-specific amount. You should know exactly what you're required to accomplish and what your rewards are.

The general rule is that ghostwriters and especially those with a new name, must put themselves on the market to get jobs.

It is a time you don't want to appear unnoticed.

Ghostwriters need to be hired.

Nowadays, we believe that the majority of people is educated, but this isn't the case. A lot of people leave school unprepared to read or write enough to create their own personal story. A few of them may be able to lead life-changing and interesting lives, and may, in the future would like to see their life experiences recorded. The need for an editor.

In all the individuals who are able to write and read, most would struggle by the thought of writing something more imaginative than a shopping list, or the occasional thank-you note. Actually, the previous time people had written more than a page two during school, however, that shouldn't deter them from coming up with ideas. If they were to come up with an idea for a story short, an entire novel, or to record their own life story and would like help, they could turn to an editor or ghostwriter to help.

In the past, my kids received mail from their grandma. They wanted to stay contact with us even though we were thousands of miles apart, yet she could not communicate her feelings in writing. Once the letters came in, we knew exactly the message before we even opened the envelope. It was all the same almost word-for-word. The joke was about her photographing these and putting the most recent one of them in an envelope every week. While we were there, she would have a lot of stories she could tell her grandkids. They could relate stories, but she was convinced that she was incapable to write them down.

It is easy for us to write ideas on paper, however we're the best of them, the writers. There are many who have stories that they want to share but cannot put the words down on paper or onto a screen. Examples include:

* Violet was bombed from her house during wartime and enlisted in the WAAF and was taught how to manage barrage balloons.

* Dennis was an Bantam an regiment consisting of soldiers who were unable to attain the height of the norm that is 5'3. He was wounded and fought in WWI and also lost his battles along with his.

A lot of ordinary folks have faced major challenges and led challenging, enjoyable and fascinating lives. It's true that everybody has a book within them, and this is usually the case. Every one of us has the written record of our lives. There are many individuals would love to have their own narrative written down, and they have some great tales to share however for some reason or another, they are unable to create them their own sake. The stories that follow generations will love reading. There's an enormous desire to learn about genealogy, looking into the past, and building family tree. Everybody would like to know the origins of their family and why they are the person they have become. Perhaps there's not enough information for to write a book but there's enough data to create some interesting pieces for a magazine of specialized interest like a genealogy journal or even some of the gray market magazines, specifically those geared toward those over 50.

That's why our abilities as writers are very appreciated. If someone isn't able to compose their own tales, we're able to help the person.

There's a big difference between having an idea of what you wish to convey and the ability to put your phrases on paper. Examples:

The young man has been invited to be the most important man in the wedding of his friend. He is aware of how much his friendship means to him, and he is full of funny stories that he would like to share with the guests. However, when he sits down to create his speech, he doesn't have a clue where to start. The need for the help of a ghostwriter.

The young lady was a victim of a horrific experience, but she has come through and is now determined to inform all of the people in the country, and the world at large, of her experience. English was one of her most challenging subjects at school. She has no clue how to write her thoughts down with the black-and-white. The writer she needs is an assistant ghostwriter.

I had a conversation with a lady who wanted to know how I could present a manuscript she was working on to submit to publishers. "I've sent a certain person a proposal and she told me and they wanted for the complete manuscript. The information she gave me later was shocking. She sent her proposal to the publisher over twenty years ago. I was skeptical that her publishers could be able to remember her and her ideas even after all this time. If I inquired why it took so long, she confessed to loving her subject matter, however she was not keen on the writing aspect. The writer should have requested to have a ghostwriter assist her when the business has expressed an interest in her proposition.

Write down notes. Take a notepad and pen, and then quickly note as many stories of family members' or friends interesting stories that you imagine. You have five minutes. Ask yourself if the people in the story would prefer to have their tales published If they do you can split the proceeds together with the writer.

It's busy, bustling

If someone else has information but doesn't have the expertise or experience, a ghost writer is able to write about their expert areas to them. Examples:

A businessman who is successful would like to write his own personal story.

He is certainly likely to write about it, but if he could only find the opportunity. Therapists want to record their profession, and

share knowledge with others.

Each requires the services of a ghostwriter. If you've never owned dogs doesn't mean you shouldn't be able to write a book on a particular breed. If you're a fan of snack foods like crisps, chocolate and junk food, that doesn't hinder the possibility of writing about good nutrition. Clients provide you with the details and you write on paper the information.

A lot of people who have tales that relate to their life, ideas and experiences, or businesses have too much on their plate to take the time to sit down long enough to create a book. It's possible that they don't possess the time or desire to do it, but are eager to have an account of their company or their expertise, such as the best way to manage the hotel or what they think on the power of positive thought. They'd love to have their name printed on the cover. They've got information they can give, but they don't have the expertise to be able to impart it. What are they able to do? Search for someone who possesses the abilities. That's us! The company hires a ghostwriter to create the content for them.

I can't write, and won't write.

Many people don't know how to write on paper. They lack the words to speak their mind. You can watch a television personality interviewing them and it is clear. Consider how often the word "basically" is mentioned in the interview and you'll know what I'm talking about. The conversation may be cliche but we never write about their words are you? Maybe, but we'd use their voices, but we'd aim to create a more sophisticated sound and edit out the repeated use of the well-known phrases.

The interview for the job

Are you an actual ghost? Other than being a dejected person that was hoping to read ghost stories on these pages, who in the absence of haunting, spend the time they had writing I'm betting you're an author. Perhaps you write in one of the type of genre like romance, fiction stories, historical epics, or maybe you write short things like articles, features, or stories. If you haven't been released yet, or your CV is spread over multiple sheets of A4 you might want to explore something new, or try an entirely different approach and even ghost. If you have not been published up until now, this could become your strength. Anyone who is able to get into a story or connect with the other people could be considered an escapist. Anyone who loves discovering new subjects could be a ghost. Try answering the questions below to determine if you're ghostwriter-worthy.

Do you have the ability to write?

* Can you write quickly?

Are you the kind of writer that says "yes" initially and then wonders

later?

Are you ready to face any challenge?

* Do you like the people around you?

* Do you enjoy exploring new ideas?

If you've answered "yes" to all of the questions above, then you're half way there.

Are you able to write?

You will definitely require the ability to. The skills you will require are ones that a large portion of us aren't aware of or have forgotten: grammar, punctuation and a clearly and precisely way of communicating your thoughts.

Take note of if you're still not one hundred percent 100 percent certain of your grammar or punctuation, then purchase a book that covers this topic (Perfect Grammar Derek Soles, Studymates).

Can you write quickly?

Being able to write quickly is an important benefit. There are some jobs that may require today. Some will need to be completed immediately. It could take a while to write a story however the earlier you take on the task and get it completed, then you'll be ready begin the next task.

Are you the kind of writer that says "yes" at first but thinks later?

The majority of serious writers aren't able to decline assignments. A lot of my writing buddies accept without hesitation when they are asked to write anything or any thing. The rule of caution does not apply to writing for money or a income.

Chapter 9: Are you ready to take on any challenge?

There are certain subjects that I'd not choose to avoid, pornography is one. If you are afflicted by fear of spiders and you are required to write a novel for the benefit of a spider expert, it may be logical to refuse. But, on the other hand, taking on the issue could provide a means of overcoming your fears.

If the activity is ethical, legal and fascinating, take it on. Don't be frightened. Fear can take away a lot of the excitement.

Note down your subjects that you wouldn't wish to write on. Which topics do you find offensive? What are you not at ease with?

Do you like people?

Writers are usually fascinated by the people around them. They're the ones who sit watching from the sidelines during parties. The writers can be friendly, however whenever a brand new character (person) comes into their lives it is likely that they'll be those who ask all the questions. Writers should be aware of how non-writers think. If they spot an individual waiting at the bus station and are left wondering which direction they're going to or why they're not and what's in their bags. They hear a line in a conversation and are eager to learn every detail. Writers are interested in knowing about people's lives as well as their passions, love stories, triumphs and failures, their children or careers ... The question is, in simple terms, are you observant? If you're not to be curious, do you have a keen interest in the world?

Are you keen to discover something new?

Writers are instructed to record what they've learned but this doesn't mean they can't benefit from learning something new. A while ago, I was asked to write a piece on property in a local paper. The good news is that I was employed by an institution of building at the period, and when the managing took a break for lunch, I'd go to his office to look through his documents in search of any bits and pieces which might be useful. Then, in a matter of a few months, I was a pro at mortgages, insurances and even the housing market as a whole. To learn something new, it requires calling experts, conducting research and studying. All of these are not challenging, and some are even hard. If a beekeeper is required to write a report on the business he runs and later wants you to complete the work for him, you should not hesitate because all you've learned about bees is they are black and yellow stripes, and that they bite. The person you are working with will provide all the details you require, or perhaps most of it, while your research will take care of the remainder. Be wary of minor things like lack of understanding. The ability to learn is there and it is incredibly fascinating to learn the process of reflexology, what women were fighting for their right to vote, how to create a thousand and one things using lavender, or the background of bicycles. The subjects you've never considered may end up being extremely fascinating.

The abilities required by ghostwriters

The ability you have is already there to write. You may have to improve is interviewing abilities. This will be discussed in Chapter 5. this in Chapter 5. It is also important to appear and sound as professional. You shouldn't appear like you've just climbed off the couch. Make sure you check your reflection before going out. Does the reflection you are looking at resemble someone you'd want to reveal the secrets of your life to or ask to create a self-help guide or an engineering guide?

If you're worried, you should do what I do and apply the " As If ' principle. The idea is to act as if can be confident, competent and confident and successful. It's effective. I guarantee it. I've been doing this for many years.

Be aware that your customer may be just the same way as you. Your job is to set them at ease, so that they feel comfortable with them and be able to trust them to trust. It is essential that you appear confident, professional and confident. If you find it hard then take a deep breath and repeat to yourself "Relaxed, cool, calm and confident. That's how I did when I first started interviewing people.

What does a ghostwriter need?

Forget ego here. Ghostwriters are practically unnoticed and the vast majority of them are not even known. If you're planning to write about topics which appeal to you, then writing ghost isn't the right way to proceed. If you're hoping to display your work or sign books in large stores, ghostwriting will not do this for you.

Working hard

Working hard is a result of practicing. You can take a couple of weeks from writing, and you'll be getting back to the drawing board once you return to the task. You're feeling rusty and don't feel satisfied with the work you've produced however, keep going and the skills will come back. Just like riding a bike, they can't be lost.

Take note of - schedule your time to allow you the time to promote the ghostwriting aspect of your writing company in addition to the time to actually write.

Don't be patient waiting to see the Muse. The Muse is always in holiday mode. In the beginning of any endeavor, it's the beginning which is the toughest. This blank page is the initial step. After you've started, you'll be wondering what the issue is. I guarantee it. I'm a professional writer.

Henry Ford was supposed to say to his son "The harder you work the luckier you get." The more you put in on the field of publishing the more you get your name everywhere and that's precisely the thing you'd like to achieve.

In my early years as a mom, I started writing thoughts of the gasoline bill as well as school uniforms, and brand new shoes constantly motivated me to create and market stories. An acquaintance has created a conservatory that is, she has the material was sold to fund the construction of a new conservatory at her house.

For readers outside the UK: A lot of UK houses have conservatories, which is an area that is extended into the garden, typically from to the side of the house. The majority of them are made of glass and, when the weather isn't warm enough to lounge out in the open, it is a wonderful way to take in sunlight and light.

If money is a motivator to make you feel better, then become materialistic. It's not necessary to inform who you are. They should think that it's just passion and love, not only the shady glamour.

The shock effect

The ghosts of books have been rumored to be on paedophilia and child abuse brutal real-life murders, or even sexual incest. It doesn't matter what, someone is victimized. Some of these victims victim or perpetrators would like to record their experience. If they reach out to you, it is important to think about consideration to whether you'd like to write about their story and if you would prefer not to. If the subject is likely to frighten or irritate you or violate your moral values, think twice. You are entitled to refuse. ('It's extremely kind for you to inquire about me, but I'm obliged to be polite in the case of murder.)

The book I first wrote for a ghostwriter was only a quarter-finished draft after my client made a shocking revelation. Her husband was implicated in a crime that was both illegal and inhumane and tragic. What could I do? To stop all the time the effort and time I that I put into this project or behave like an experienced journalist and go back to work? I chose to do the latter. It was difficult for me to listen to they were also difficult to record, but the novel was finished and was the story of my client including wrinkles and all. The book was a deserved 10 out of 10 for her total, and sometimes brutal sincerity.

The profile of a successful ghostwriter

Thus, we've identified the characteristics of a competent ghostwriter. They're insatiable about places, people and, obviously, their the subjects they write about. They love writing and write with ease. They're not afraid and are passionate about writing. Does this sound similar to you? Even if you're not able to master one or two of the traits, they could be developed through experience and practice.

I have a writer friend who could make a great ghostwriter. She's curious about individuals. She is always asking questions whenever she has a conversation with somebody new. She is able to remember the name of someone. She is extremely curious regarding everyone. If you meet her after some time, and you're likely to be asked questions.

An additional string is attached to the bow

In the freelancing world, it's not a good idea to rely on just only one or two markets. The editors of magazines shift, and consumers' needs shift. Recently, a lot of women's magazines have stopped publishing fiction. These magazines employ personnel to create special features. It's good to receive money in a variety of directions rather than relying solely on the same or two channels. Expand your horizons as a professional author. Consider writing in genres that you haven't previously tried. It's possible that they will surprise and excite you. Ghostwriting might be among them.

Remember that ghosts will be the money for their work, regardless of whether the piece is printed or it doesn't. It is your decision to set a cost and then draft the contract prior to starting. See Chapter 4. The idea of selling and getting paid for your work without being required to do so is risky that may not result in the money you need. Ghostwriting could be performed alongside normal work or even while creating your bestseller novel.

"I'm thrilled to be able to use my knowledge of storytelling to bring a story to life. I am thrilled that they appreciate the work I perform for them. It's also much more stable as a method for earning money as fiction writing appears to be today. In addition, I'm developing a second novel.'

Lynne Barrett-Lee www.lynnebarrett-lee.com

If you are a writer to earn a living or just to earn additional money, then writing for ghosts is an additional way to earn money from your writing. The only thing you have to look for is the outlet and clients, which means creating your own company. Chapter Two will explain the steps to take.

Note down if you're seriously considering ghostwriting and you want to be a great reporter, you should constantly be looking for stories that are interesting.

Opportunities to write a ghost

There are many potential opportunities to be watching out in the process of starting a business. Each of these could require the help of the help of a ghostwriter.

* A famous person who would like to have their autobiography published.

The average person is looking to write their autobiography, or memoirs written.

The average person is able to share a story.

* A blogger that wants his or her posts to be enjoyable as well as informative.

Professionals who want to have their specialization written but isn't able to do it them.

• A webmaster that wants to stand out but isn't sure of what to write about.

*Anyone who must make a presentation but is nervous.

* A famous person who has an idea to write a book.

A common person who may have an idea for the creation of a novel.

A young person seeking a romantic love poem to his partner and vice versa.

* Publishers who want to publish a book or books, to be written by a ghostwriter for the author that does not exist.

A business that wants their products to be featured in a blog, advertised or even written about.

Locally based person who is knowledgeable about local people, places, buildings etc. however, does not possess the capability of writing about it for themselves.

Things to keep in mind

* If you're able to write you are able to write for ghostwriters.

There's a massive marketplace for freelance writers.

Everybody has a story, but not all of them has the ability to write their

story.

The ability to stretch yourself through tackling diverse subjects will

Enhance your writing abilities and enhance the quality of your CV.

2. Establishing a business

One minute overview

In this chapter

Sucking eggs

- A space to conduct interviews with prospective clients.

They find you They find you Searching for potential clients

Real-life celebrity

Information from the internet

Chapter 10: How to convince people to join

Sucking eggs

In the beginning, I would like to offer sorry if been through this at many different places and are aware of that you're in the right place. It is my request to be patient and think about this short piece of information a brief summary on the things you should know in order to be successful.

If ghostwriting is will be a minor portion of your writing career, you'll still have to remain professional when it comes to writing. Think of it as a enterprise. It's a good thing that it can begin with only a small cost. There's a good chance you have everything you require.

Tools to use

If you're not an absolute beginner, there's an internet-connected computer. Additionally, you will have necessary equipment that needed by a writer to get started: a phone, a printer and paper, spare inkjets or printer ink cartridges pen, and the filing system.

Additionally, you require exposure, writing abilities as well as clients and the capacity to put in the work. If you are a writer, you likely already possess all of those things, however you may consider adding an audio recorder, and ideally with a digital version add it to your wish list. These devices are extremely useful for interviewing customers.

Take note of your shopping list - make with a list of items to buy and then be sure to have all the items you require.

Work from home

Also, you'll need an office. In the case of office, it doesn't mean you have to go out in a hurry and lease one. Office can be defined as a place where you can write.

You must be off from distractions, but others can work in noisy cafés, rooms, or train stations. It is possible to complete your writing as you travel to work by train. If, as I am, you're looking for a spot for yourself, you should find one quickly. The corner of your bedroom, an area at the highest point of the stairs in the attic, basement, the shed, summerhouse or anywhere it is possible to shut yourself off and enjoy some time to yourself. Even if you only take notes on your sofa or in breaks during work, or during breaks at your "proper" job, you have to find a space to put your notes.

Take note of it that it's best to clean up your workspace prior to beginning an exciting new venture.

The perfect place to conduct interviews with clients

Is it your property or someone else's? Perhaps somewhere else? Should you be thinking of interviewing your customers from your personal

Home owners must consider a comfy home for your home.

that you are able to do. In your view you're probably able to do this.

The most efficient way to get your work done.

The beginning stages of your partnership with your customer

It's best to bring someone else into the living space to share the house with it's a good idea to have someone else in the house with.

Maybe you could ask your partner/sister/whoever to answer

you open the doors to your client. It will let the client be aware that you are at

You aren't alone.

Do not invite clients to the mess of a room with books are piled up and

documents must be moved before sitting at your table. You must organize sure you have your

Relaxing interviewing environment because when the interviewer isn't calm, you aren't going to be able to get the most out of the interviewer. You must make them feel welcome. You can make them feel at ease. Pour them a cup tea. Ask them questions, or preferring, let them to speak.

Note down the dates - You must decide on what part of your home that you'll interview in. Make sure it is tidy, and certain that your interviewer and you do not get disturbed.

For some customers, your house might not be the right place. Ghostwriters can book an hotel room to stay for a couple of days with clients. They in that time, gather all the data they require for the project. Of course, this will not always be possible. The cost of living must be taken into consideration.

Others clients may be happier having their interview conducted in their personal workplace, particularly if the assignment is to write about their company or the success in achieving fame and wealth. If they're busy, they might prefer this.

If you're looking for a short time-based ghosting job like speeches or brief article, a coffee shop might work for your needs. Be aware that the voice recorder can take in all the background noise. There's also an opportunity that once returned to your workstation the recording will prove to be ineffective.

Offering your products or

One time that ghostwriters have to be the front of the pack in advertising their services. It's called exposure.

There is no doubt that you will require the web and a blog. If you're one of those who enjoys being to Twitter or Facebook during short intervals of time instead to spending a large chunk of time alone mucking around with the platforms, consider these also. Writing forums online are an additional opportunity to advertise your writing business.

Websites

The website must be current. Clients may permit them to showcase the work you performed for them, and this could become your storefront. It is also possible for sale of books written by clients on your site. Make a copy of your current CV and upload it to your website. Include all the tasks that you've completed, however, in the event that your client has committed your confidentiality, be sure that you're not precise about the work you performed on behalf of the client. Make sure that your website is professional. Make sure you double-check grammar and spelling errors. Also, ask a third party to look it over too. Do you think that you would trust an untruthful person if you looked up their website but discovered it was full of errors or grammar errors, as well as incorrect spelling?

Someone who needed assistance with her writing was referred to me via my site. The time was when I hadn't mentioned in the website that I'd undertake ghostwriting assignments, but my ghostwritten book was listed on the site. My hobbies were included and it is the main reason she decided to go with me. We both shared the same passion and she believed that I could make the ideal character for her.

Consider listing the hobbies you enjoy and passions in your About Me section. There is no way to know if someone will need your ghostwriting services because of your love in making potpourri or an obsession with hanging-gliding. Make sure to add any fields that you're experts in.

Take note of this - If there isn't a site for your business and you don't have the knowledge to create one by yourself, you should look for somebody who could help you. Look at your friends and family before looking to find someone who is willing to get paid.

Take note of - If you're serious about to write for others, then inform everyone about it. Visit your site and be sure that you're notifying everyone that you're open to doing this type of assignments. It should be easy for them to get in touch with you by providing a the link to contact you via email.

Emails

Include a signature on any emails that offer your ghostwriting service. It is as easy as selecting Tools, followed by Options, Signatures, New and. After that, type what you would like to write and then tick the Add to all messages outgoing. Apply. Okay, you're done. Make sure to change your signature if needed. You can delete the service if have other commitments and are not looking to find writing projects.

Add to the conclusion of your emails all books that you would like to offer on behalf of your clients.

Get in touch with everyone on your address book, and tell them about your services as a ghostwriter.

Traditional advertising

If you are looking for more conventional ways to get your company recognized, you could consider placing a few ads in magazines that are appropriate. If, for instance, you're interested in writing stories to older folks, you can try any of the "grey market" magazines. They are designed for people who are over 50. They also have ads for writing services like editing, research and ghostwriting.

Make a small postcard advertisement that you can place on any display you can. There are some supermarkets with boards where local businesses can showcase their merchandise. Libraries are equipped with boards that advertise occasions, events, and clubs as well as services. Be on the lookout for possibilities.

Note down - let other libraries around the area be aware of your business as a ghostwriter but not just that closest to you. Choose the your area that you'll be willing to take on. How far would you like to be able to

Business cards for business

Always have your business cards on you whenever you take your business cards. Keep all your contact details in them, and also list your offerings. If you have already listed you as an independent writer or creative writing instructor, then you should create a new set with ghostwriters included. Do not ever leave home with your business cards in give out. Have a couple in your purses and pockets as well as shopping bags. When you travel, make certain to bring your credit cards.

Be sure to keep them simple and straight to the point. Beware of fancy fonts that could cause difficulty to comprehend. Do not try to think of clever ways by adding pictures, in particular these tiny quills and inkpots that are favored by writers who've not used the tools, or ever seen these in person. Your card should be easy to read, straightforward and exact.

Note down when you'll have business cards printed. Make sure they are clear and straight to the point. Your offering is ghostwriting.

Local papers

When you've gotten one or two commissions You can try reaching out to local newspaper to inquire whether they're interested in having an interview with your. Ghostwriting seems so interesting that it's unlikely they'll decline your offer.

Press release

Publishing a Press Release is an easy way to make sure your message gets in the public domain. In the beginning, you'll require some information. The odds are that newspapers will release an announcement about starting a business as a ghostwriter, but If you've got a specific story, notify all local media inform them of the news. A special event could be an excellent subject, so if you're presenting a lecture be sure to let the media know and inform them that the talk is concerning your role as a writer.

Journalists read news releases that they get and put them in the form of news stories. If you've performed a great job but not written more than a few words, the release might be published without any modifications however it's likely that it'll be edited and cut in order to fill in a need.

Make a Press Release about you and distribute it to each newspaper, local magazine, and radio station within the area that you are at ease working in the ten, twenty 50, 100 miles. The choice is yours.

The release needs to state everything it says on the front page. Make sure to create something that is attention attractive. Then in the body of your publication, include all the pertinent information the newspaper would require. If you make it intriguing enough, it could result in a message and possibly be contacted for additional information or perhaps a picture.

On the back the press release, write the date when it is made available for release. It could be, for instance, on the day that the book you mentioned goes available or one week before you speak. If your announcement isn't time specific, then write for immediate announcement. It should be followed by the contact information for your company: name and address, telephone (home as well as mobile) and email address, as well as or fax. There should be no reason that they aren't capable of contacting you. Make sure you stick to the one A4 side. Journalists are very busy.

Here's a sample of a press release.

Press Release

Sandra Smith

I'm A Ghost!

One night only Sandra Smith is going to be revealed to the world. Sandra is ghostly. Sandra has been spotted in booksellers during the book signings are taking place, but Sandra doesn't sign books. Her name won't be on the spine of any book. Sandra is an author-in-residence. The stories she writes for her clients and she writes the text.

"Being a ghostwriter, I'm able to take on a variety of life experiences,' Sandra says. Sandra"and in this event, I'll talk about certain subjects that I've wrote about. They include fascinating tales of life, a novel about Feng Shui written on behalf of an expert on this field, and an award-winning novel that has the name of an iconic actor on the front cover.

Sandra will speak on My Life As A Ghost in The Studio Theatre, Any Street, Any Town, starting at 8pm on Thursday, 4th August.

Tickets can be purchased at the box offices. Prices start from PSx. expires

To allow immediate release.

If you require additional information, please email Mrs Sandra Smith, address, phone numbers, fax number and email.

Note down - write your own press release. Also, write down all the addresses you're able to imagine sending the message to.

Radio stations

A Press Release may be delivered for radio broadcasting. Radio stations in the local area are constantly seeking interesting people and this includes you as the ghostwriter. The audience will be interested to learn more about the work of a ghost. Ghost's very name can entice the listener enough to keep them tuned in. What is more fascinating than watching a ghost live on air? It is certain that the station will savor this word for all it's value.

Talks

Writers Did you give talks as a writer? It's another method to reach out and inform people that you provide a service. Invite a speaker to the Writers' Circles in your local area. Women's Institutes, Probus Clubs various society and clubs are looking for engaging speakers. Discuss with a group the idea of ghostwriting. There might be people in the crowd that needs your help. The majority of the group will return home to inform a friend about your services. Then your name is spread. News spreads, and new jobs start to come in.

My first client, a personal experience

My first client came across me through a writer's group and a library. We'll call her Susan. Susan was in the middle of a kiss-and-tell story to tell, and she wanted someone to compose it down for her. She was aware that the task was way beyond her abilities, so she started searching for help. She contacted her library in the area and inquired whether they had any information on ghostwriters. They did not, but they did direct her to the nearby Writers' Circle. Susan received an email address for the secretary. She contacted the secretary and was told that they didn't have any experienced people to do the job. (They may have, but no one would be willing to risk it and do something completely new.) They suggested a different group that she could reach out to and they gave the woman a number. It was my number.

Note down - let the other writing groups within the area you are in your skills as a ghostwriter and you're ready to tackle the task.

Chapter 11: The Three-Foot-Rule

A sales tactic is known as the Three-Foot-Rule. It was discovered by me during an excursion to one of the large American firms that tell you that it's possible to make thousands from your time selling their products.

The Three-Foot-Rule is not changed to metric since The Metre Rule doesn't have the identical ring. Three-Foot Rule is a simple rule of thumb. Three Foot Rule means exactly the same thing as it states. If you're within three feet of someone, you must sell to the person. It is suggested that you talk to them at a party, bus stop, in a medical waiting room and then talk about the service you're selling. This is the case with ghostwriting. For me, as a writer, it's about shifting the conversation to tasks. If you ask them what they do, they'll reply, 'And you?' Tell that you're a freelance writer. If you're a writer, they'll be interested in knowing your name, and then ask whether they know who you are. Ghostwriters don't be expecting to learn your name, but you might need to explain the idea of ghostwriting.

According to my research Nine percent of the time someone you've met will say they've always dreamed of writing books and many say "When I've got time." Find out what kind of book they'd like create and, if the idea is promising, ask them to help them with it. Inform them of the way they'll put their name on the front cover and, if they'd like to, they'll be required to swear off any secrets. Give them your professional card. It's unlikely that they will take it back, however a tiny percentage of them may think about it and call you back later. A tiny percentage is more effective than none even if it's not even a fraction of a percent.

The Three-Foot-Rule should not be used by people who don't have the courage to take on challenges. adding your brand to the discussion can be tricky. However, when they do come up, make sure that you're prepared. Don't be shy and make yourself known.

Publishers and agents

If you've got a resume with some examples of work that you have ghosted, you can try contacting agents and editors. The people who are looking to write books often approach agents asking for advice. If an agent knows more about the person you are and also your passions then you may be able to find some work. If you're not able to be recognized by anyone who has any idea what you're up to, it's unlikely that you'll achieve anything.

Chriss McCallum shares her tale.

"I was invited to attend an event in Manchester together with about 30 others from the Society of Authors. The group was from an extensive area, and we'd all replied to an email sent by the Society to find out if anybody was looking to write a ghost story. The gathering was organized through an agency who'd received numerous requests from the public on how to find ghostwriters. Agents were also working together with a number of staff in the English department at Manchester University. After registering an interest at the conference and later being contacted by the agent who offered an opportunity to write a novel.'

Journalist Jane Bidder, says, "I was approached by an expert who'd received a request from a publishing house to create a book about the subject he was specialized in. The expert was busy and didn't have time and, since I'd conducted interviews with him previously and asked the editor to let me be his writer.'

"For my very first piece",' explains Zoe King, 'I was invited because I was already a participant in The Society of Women Writers & Journalists.'

I was employed by the company that provided correspondence training for authors. In the event that the company decided to provide a self-publishing option, I was approached for assistance after being asked by an officer looking for somebody to write his biography.'

Janie Jackson-Julia Anderson was in many years of waiting before she got her first gig as a ghostwriter. "I'd said two years ago that I'd have a chance to test writing ghost stories in the future,' she says and twenty years later, I got a call to ghostwrite the pages of a book. The writer had spent 15 years writing what was later revealed to be the basic outlines of the novel.'

Lynne Barrett-Lee was contacted by an ex-husband's patients. She had read my writing and was a fan of my newspaper columns,' she says. 'She suggested that I help to write her tale.'

Organizations and groups

If you're not a part of any organization or writing group, then join one now. You must meet certain requirements to being a member of for the Society of Authors or the Society of Women Writers and Journalists. Most likely, you already have the necessary qualifications for joining one or both. Other organizations that could be beneficial. Check out the Writers' and Artists' Yearbook (A&C Black) for additional information.

Find them, they discover you.

If you continue to promote your services as a ghostwriter for a long time, enough, clients will eventually reach out to your. It's not an easy task to start an entirely new venture and it can require time to set up. Be persistent and continue to tell people about your business and let people know how they can reach your.

Networking

A majority of customers will approach your location, but there's nothing wrong by going out looking for one your own. Networking is a term used to describe it. It means that you must move around, present your personality and network with other persons who may be of use for you. Do you think that sounds awful? It's more fun to consider networking as creating new friendships. This certainly is.

Since I started writing, I joined a writing group that attended all workshops that was advertised locally standing in the bookstores and libraries whenever authors spoke, and was a delegate to conferences and, applying the concept of "As If that I applied, I behaved as were I didn't feel one bit anxious at the prospect of meeting all these amazing people who achieved the goal I wanted to achieve--being in print. I smiled, and spoke to them. I am able to claim that I didn't meet a author who resisted or refused to talk to me.

Don't only connect with writers. Being a ghost-aspiring writer, you must network everywhere you travel. This could include your golf course, food store crowd, the garden centre ... The greater the number of people you interact with then the more effectively you will promote yourself as ghostwriters and the greater chances of receiving commissions. Ghostwriters should be present in the background after they've completed a customer's book. It is possible that they won't even attend book events when the author fears they may be able to give away the game. Ghosts must be visible while looking for jobs.

Since your potential writer is not likely to be aware of the nuances of the publishing industry It is crucial for you to stay on top of the latest developments in the publishing industry. That's why networking is crucial. Make sure you do as many networking events as could, no matter if it's through writing groups like SWWJ, The Society of Authors and so on. as well as through writers' conventions. Be sure to keep your eyes on the writing press like Writers' News and Writers' Forum.'

Zoe King www.zoeking.com Make a note of Network networks and network

In search of clients

Everybody has a book within their lives. False or true? The reason I believe it's the case is because every person has their own personal events to record. There are some who will be much better than others, but every person's story is significant for them, and a lot of people want to have their own story written.

Searching for famous people

Who do you know? Are there famous people in your area? Are you acquainted with or will you see someone who's performed at the theatre, or taken part in a tour across the country or even appeared on TV? Be on the lookout for occasions to get in touch with celebrities.

I was a guest on the popular game show on television, Deal Or No Deal, and became famous even for a brief duration. A journalist contacted me to ask whether he would be able to write my tale. Naturally, I'd published it in a number of magazines, however, after I told him I was able to write about my personal experiences, the writer graciously provided me with the contact number of the editor whom he'd pushed through the concept to and was willing to create my own story. If the journalist had collaborated on the story, it could have been a "as told to" piece that could have been called "Lynne's Big Win, as told to an unnamed Freelance'. If I, or the freelance writer who was not named and a writer that was in the show, we might write about the experience of they and their name. We could both have ghostwritten the other person.

Maybe a person you know is a winner of Lotto and Euromillions or another lottery near where you reside. You will likely be featured in the headlines and will be categorized at some point as a celeb. It is possible that there's a background to their victory, such as the fact that they were bankrupt and lost their house just prior to winning. it could be you as the ghost writer who relates their story.

The kind of information you see is usually found in local newspapers. The newspaper will report on what happened but it is possible to make it an engaging piece for a magazine through the emotions or experiences the person who was involved. The piece could be classified as an interview, if you add your identity on it. However, most individuals, when asked, prefer their names on the piece as well as for other people to believe that they wrote it by themselves.

It is rare to be living next to a famous film actor or an established name on TV, however, you may have a connection with someone. Keep your ears peeled when your auntie informs you that the next neighbor's son was in an West End show, inquire whether it is possible to visit him.

You never know, he could consider having his own script written, and you could be on his radar when it is time. It is often luck that has to do having the ability to be just in the right spot in the right moment at the right timing.

Are you looking for heroes of every day life?

You can read these stories in your local paper or read reports from the other side. A local hero fights off family flames reads the headline and the actual facts about the incident are out there for everyone to see. Ghosts are tasked with be able to get into the mind of the protagonist and then write an article about his or perhaps the book.

Take note of the newspaper you read every week, and then check the paper for any possible job opportunities as a ghostwriter.

There are bound to be a lot of people who are interesting within your community, but they're not likely to be household names. Take a look at all the contacts that you've made through the different areas in your life. People who share similar sports, hobbies and passions like you. Individuals who have succeeded or suffered through and overcome challenges, or even have cheated the death.

You are looking for family-related stories

I'm currently writing the family's history to write a story for our son. A lot of grandparents wish to write similar. Nearly all grandparents as well as great-grandparents may want their family's story documented. I'm able to write my own. Can they write their own? It's probably not.

Be aware and pay attention to the elderly individuals. My mom lived in a shelter and every person was a character with a tale to share. The residents had all survived conflict, for instance. But were there other hidden treasures in their histories?

My father-in-law worked as an engineer, which was one of the occupations that were reserved for during wartime. He believed he didn't do his part for the King and Country, however, a few years later after his death the friend he had with him informed us of how he'd carried explosives in his bag in the event of an air attack. Unaware of what could befall him, he reversing the train to ensure it was in a safe tunnel. Do you think he no idea to talk about the incident to anyone?

There are plenty of tales such as my father-in-law's. These stories belong to people who live on the streets, everyday individuals who aren't aware that they've accomplished anything that is out from the norm. They aren't proud of their heroic feats, but should you be able to locate the people, they might inform you of their experiences and permit the writer to publish their story regardless of whether for an article or book. The collection might be fascinating and it's up to you to get those words in the minds of contributors. It is your job to listen to their stories and then make them come alive.

Chapter 12: The unwritten stories of all time

I knew a person named Christina. She was an early female motorcycle driver in The Second World War. I had no idea until her death and the fact was revealed at the funeral. Since then I've been wondering about the stories she told. Hopefully, she passed them on to the children and grandchildren of her. It would be terrible for them to die together, however, how many others did this occur to?

The next time you're in the middle of a busy town check out. Each person that you pass by tells a story.

* A mother of a severe handicapped child might form a support group for others who are struggling with the same or may be on the front of a charitable organization that raises money to study the condition the child was born.

* The boy carrying a rucksack could be taking a trip to travel around the globe.

* A couple looking through the windows of a bicycle shop could be set trying to set a record riding across John O'Groats to Land's End.

* The woman being watched by the store detective could be suffering from a very real disease--kleptomania. A condition that isn't understood by many, but they could be educated when you take into consideration her tale.

Watch the people passing by for about ten minutes. There is a chance that a significant portion of them will have a story worthy of writing about, whether in an article of a few lines or as a entire book. However, the vast majority that you read about wouldn't be in a position to write the story by themselves. They'd have to hire a ghostwriter. It's possible to do this for them.

Note down to always be looking for stories

Popularity in real life

There's a notion that people are all attracted to the true tales that magazines are filled with and can be seen on television screens. This is because many people do not live an old-fashioned, family-like life. It's the kind of assistance that families received in the past when all of their family members were within walking distance of one another. There was someone we could turn for help in the event of a crisis for advice, and we had the support of friends who knew us. Today, our neighbors are unknown, nameless and faceless but the characters in soaps are easy to recognize and name. They are popular due to the fact that soap family members become real to the viewers who watch to learn what's going on with the characters. It's the same with all the real life tales and programs. We love to observe what other people do. We're curious about the lives of others, but a lot of them are not able to write. This is when you can become ghostwriter. Writing about other people's lives is never going to be less popular.

A satiating craving

There have for a long time been rumors that the general public had become bored with the real-life dramatics. The sales of life stories about celebrities were expected to fall. Have you seen it? Go through the schedules on television to find out how much real-time they are using. The cameras are set up in families' residences so that viewers can observe the lives of other people. It is interesting to hear about how the victims dealt and/or didn't cope with incidents, wars and natural catastrophes, or even attacks. Teenagers share their secrets to hosts such as Jeremy Kyle, celebrities invite us to talk about their happiness as well as their struggles. Isn't that all evidence the insatiable desire for stories from the real world?

Look through the shelves of booksellers, or look through the pages of magazines You will find evidence that shows how real-life stories are as well-loved like they have ever been. There is, and likely ever will be a massive audience for these tales. No matter if they're simple, popular, daring foolish or tragic, people continue to show an intense interest in true lives tales. We humans will forever be fascinated by other people and always learn more about them or read books or articles on their lives. This is when the ghostwriter comes in.

There is a chance that you won't be able to offer your book to a big publication, but publishing just one version of the book could very easily be accomplished today. Self-publishing isn't expensive anymore and is a great answer for all grandparents that want to share their story to their grandchildren, kids as well as future generations. If a small number of copies are required, they can be made with a computer with images.

Kiss-and-tell

Numerous celebrity stories fall under the category. If a relationship fails, one or both parties often both their story to a nationwide newspaper. The wronged partner may get the creation of a book. There aren't just celebrities who are guilty of this. A lot of ordinary people might wish to get revenge by using the written word. Be cautious when deciding whether or not to agree to the possibility of such an incident as they could be the stories that could cause issues and may result in legal proceedings. If you decide to go with it, be sure to include an agreement that protects you from all statements made by the client. The client acknowledges and accepts total accountability for any legal outcome. Another option is to sign up as a business as you'll have only a limited responsibility. That means you will only be responsible to the worth of the business and consequently, in the event that you were sued, not be at risk of losing the home you live in. If you decide to become the owner of a business, you must meet strict laws that apply to your company. Therefore, you must seek advice on legal matters from a qualified expert.

Information on the internet

If you've got a day or two, you can put "ghostwriting" into a search engine, and then look through the thousands of possibilities However, beware of those who will require small amounts of money. The details are in Chapter 8.

Inspiring that the public

Consider the final product you're going to make -- a draft of a piece of work written by ghostwriters that is of a certain type. How can you convince the general public to use this service?

Everyone would like their lives to flow smoothly and effortlessly. The majority of people will admit that they don't have enough hours to complete all they want and need to accomplish. If you want to have their ideas published printed but do not have enough time or energy to create this on their own, you're providing them with time and an expert service that can help their dream be realized. The media spread an image that says anything is achievable fast and efficiently. Lose weight within four weeks, stop smoking for good in just five easy steps, and learn to swim in just one lesson. Are you able to see the most important words? Simple and easy are often featured. The other benefit is the small amount of stages or a short period of time for achieving your vision. That's what you'll offer to customers. It is possible to make the process of writing their novel simple and feasible for them to write without having to spend a lot of their precious time. It is important to convince them that they can't write without the help of the help of a ghostwriter.

It is also possible to provide the reader with compelling motives to get the memoirs of their loved ones written. It is an extremely popular pastime nowadays. There are television shows and publications on the subject. There are sites. Who doesn't want to know the stories of their family's past? If I could have the copy of my great-grandmother's biography, it would be a treasure to keep. In reality it is, I know nothing about her. Imagine a great-grandchild getting to read your stories about life.

Memoirs are great gifts to the family members and can remain in the family for many generations. If you assist someone in writing the memoirs of their life, you're helping them to make gifts. They can help to understand that family tree. They will also provide some family and social historical.

A radio interview

Here's a portion of a guest interview by a ghostwriter. Find out how they convey their message across, and also how they convince the listener --this was broadcast on the radio--that they are in need of her help.

Q: What kind of person would you hire to write a book?

A: A lot of your readers might wish to tell their stories or even might have an idea for a novel, but have no idea of where to begin. The people I work with are typically people who weren't interested in writing when they were in school and do not like writing. They're also people with the ability to create their own books or articles, but they can't get the time to do it, and even if they did they wouldn't like doing it.

Q: Do you waste time writing? Doesn't that sound like what you do?

A: No. I am a writer, and it's my favorite pastime. This is my work.

Q: And you receive nothing for it.

A: The majority times, ghostwriters do not receive recognition. Our names don't get to appear on book cover, and usually we do not attend the events for book launches and events, however ghostwriters are professional individuals. We are aware of what we can expect. Our job is to create content for clients and are compensated to do it. Our clients' names appear in the final item. An experienced ghostwriter would never think of that.

Q: Are they all the stories of life?

A: No. The subject matter can include novels tales, books for children blog posts, articles poetry, training guides, and other manuals. I'm able to create whatever you want and receding into the background and permit them to hand on the project as their personal.

Question: Will the family members and friends of the client recognize that this isn't their work? They should be able to distinguish the writing style from the written?

A A good ghost performer can alter their style in a way that makes it sound like it's spoken by the client. Our job is to get into the mind of the customer and transform into them for a brief period. If you needed filling your teeth, then you'd visit dentist. If you'd like to have your vehicle maintained, take it to garage. It is your job to leave the work to the experts. If you'd like to have writing but do not have time, or perhaps have the necessary knowledge, then it makes sense to engage an expert ghostwriter and let them write the work for you.

Tips to be remembered

There's lots of work for ghostwriters. Advertising generates positive results, and helps make your name noticed. Networking involves getting new contacts and a the opportunity to work on new projects. There are stories everywhere once you are trained to find them. for

them.

Newspapers, radio stations as well as magazines are seeking

to write stories as well. As an author in the local area, may serve as the one to write that

Story and gain exposure at the same time.

3 Before you begin

A brief overview of one minute

In this chapter

Prior to meeting with your potential client. client

Initial impressions

Understanding the facts

* Keep your mouth closed

How to spot them?

Following the first meeting

Parting the load

"Words of wisdom" to aspiring ghostwriters

In the lead up to your meeting with a prospective customer, you should meet them.

Spend a moment to think about what you're customer might want to know. Here is an email that I got from one of them brief and short and to the point.

" You stated you'd ghosted a person's tale. What is this about and how do you pay for it? What is the process for determining when payment will be made?"

Every customer wants to know what the task will cost them. Also, they need to understand what the process is about and what amount of time and effort is required from both sides for getting completed. The clients will also want to know when it'll take.

The prospective client is likely to expect that you have all the questions and offer all the relevant information because they're hiring you to be the professional. When you are leaving home to attend your first appointment, you must have these information in hand.

The biggest issue with regards to the clients' expectations for their books is that they've been misled predominantly by the media, into thinking that all authors are wealthy and that everyone receives huge advancements. They will require you to explain your publishing process to them in a gentle manner!

Meeting your prospective client

If you've made an initial contact with a potential client, it is necessary to arrange an informal conversation to talk about the project and arrangement of business like deadlines, publishers contracts, contract, and, of course, payment. If you have contacted them, it is likely that you have already heard their stories and know the person, or at least perhaps some. If they've contacted you but you haven't met it's the beginning step to the process of ghosting.

One of the most efficient ways is to schedule a face-to-face conversation. The meeting allows you to determine if you are able to get along with your client. This is your professional job and it's your responsibility to set the client at ease - even if you're anxious yourself. You must convince them that they know what you're doing even though it's your first experience.

Be sure to be at ease and sporting a pleasant smile.

* Be sure you've got pencils in the plural, just in case you run out of papers, and maybe a smaller digital recorder.

Be sure to be punctual. If you need to provide the excuse of being late it could cause a sour taste in your customer's trust in your.

Be sure that you're and are both sure about the place.

If you are familiar with the topic then it is possible to set up a time and place you find convenient for you and your partner to meet.

If you are unsure the identity of this person, be secure. Your meeting location is best if it's on a neutral surface to begin this meeting. You should meet in a location where there's lots of people in the vicinity. Cafés would be the best option.

My personal experience

A client contacted me to inquire to create an article for him. Naturally, I was interested. He asked whether I'd like to visit his home to talk about the project he was interested in conducting. I told him that I would not. The man was completely unknown to me and the idea of getting together there was not appealing. He asked him whether he was welcome to my home. It was again an no for similar motives. The suggestion I made was that we meet up in the town in a favorite restaurant that I frequent. That's what we did and the guy that we met turned out to be friendly and shy and, to my mind highly likely to be not the next mass killer. We took an open window and he ordered coffee as well as Danish cookies. This was Mistake Number One. It was not easy to take notes on sticky fingers in the Danish pastries. It is recommended to avoid eating while working. Also, I turned on a voice recorder with a mic to ensure that I had the complete recording of the discussion. This was Mistake Number Two. The sound of the customers talking, plates and cups clanging and the sound of traffic passing by nearly drowned out the voice of my customer after returning home. I replayed the recording. Don't rely on your recording device unless you are in a quiet area, which is not the ideal place when you first meet someone new.

Chapter 13: Initial impressions

According to some experts, the way we judge individuals within the first ten minutes of looking at them. Some believe that ten seconds are a significant period of time, and that our initial impressions form in a single tenth of a second and are it is not uncommon for them to change after that. Therefore, if you're one of those people that trusts their gut instincts, and feel an immediate dislike for your customer upon encountering them for the first time, should you step off from a job you've been offered? This isn't a formal way to conduct matters, but ultimately the choice lies with you. Nobody else will make the decision your decision. Based on my own experience, I've always been right with customers. If I was not happy initially, I'd be able to walk away, and not this has ever occurred. However, if you think you're able to let your personal issues aside, move into the business of doing it and be confident taking the initiative, then take the offer. Be aware that you're likely to spend many hours working with the client, so it is important establish a rapport. It is essential to establish trust between the writer and client.

Note if your initial conversation is enthralling to you or if you sense something for your customer take it to heart.

Chriss McCallum advises-- "Research, as best as you are able, how you're most likely to be able to work with your customer, and then look into their motivations why they want to write about their requirements for you to contribute. Be sure to ensure that the work is one that you are interested in and enjoy, as otherwise it may be a burden and is evident in the written work.'

Lynne Barrett-Lee experienced a variety of concerns when she first began working with collaborators. She states, "I have the most clear understanding of what I would like the reader to experience a book. I wanted to convey in the sense that, as practical it was my final say on everything of design and structure therefore we needed to hold an open discussion during which I lays down the laws I have to follow in controlling my creative process!

The initial meeting is a chance for the clients and writers the opportunity to get acquainted. At the beginning of the meeting, note down the information about your potential customer:

* Name,

* address,

* Telephone numbers: home mobile, work and fax numbers, as well as email.

This initial meeting gives the chance to understand precisely what your client would like you to accomplish. This gives you the opportunity to write down the basic idea the main idea, or outline, of the article, speech or narrative. In this instance, all you have to do is write down the basic information about the task. It is important to determine if it is something that would interest you. It's not the right time to dive deep into the "cradle-to-grave" story of your client's existence However, you need sufficient information to ensure that you take a shrewd decision. An easy speech to the father of the bride's wedding might seem like a straightforward task, however if there's a bit dispute between two families, you'd require to know.

"I was once aware that a potential client was still involved in a dispute between a family member over an undisputed will according to Chriss McCallum. He wanted me to write his own version of what his work was being handled by! I didn't feel like I was ready to become involved in a situation like the situation, so I turned away the offer.'

Lynne Barrett-Lee resigned from one job very young stage.

We were certain that we weren't going to meet. The customer had written her novel and had been looking for a publisher to release it for years. The book was as dry as dust to read, yet it was an amazing tale, and I was able to see immediately the way I could make it come to the world. It was obvious immediately, but she was not interested in) to be a ghostwriter because she was enthralled by what she had done although she'd received many rejections, and numerous suggestions for what she could do to improve her work, and also in addition, she didn't want) to share her feelings and share her deep emotions (she'd suffered a devastating emotional trauma). Instead, she would like to think about the facts and demonstrate her (undoubted) confidence in the in the face of these. I attempted to explain that it's a human story/the emotions people identify with and would like to know more about However, she was extremely secretive and couldn't accomplish it. This is a huge regret.'

If you're unsure of accepting the task, give your self time to think the issue over. I would not advise you to take a notebook on your person. Then you can declare that you'll need to check your diary regularly and check the amount of work you have to do. You should promise to respond to your potential client within a specified number of days. "I'll let you know tomorrow," can suffice. Lack of a diary can be a helpful tool for people who answer yes right away and afterwards regret it. It is possible that you are taking on an enormous amount of work so a snap either or the best idea. Inform the potential client that you're required to determine whether you are able to give them the attention they merit before making a commitment.

However, if you're desperate to start a ghostwriting career and eager to begin with your first venture, you must make it an appealing one to you even to a lesser extent. The time you spend is valuable. Avoid wasting your time attempting to finish something you do not have an passion for or which doesn't pay you enough. If you aren't sure that it is for you decide to say no, and search for another option that is appealing to you.

Note down if you are in doubt about whether you'd like this job, give yourself time to consider the possibilities. Do not feel pressured to make the decision in a hurry.

Finding the truth

Consider asking at the initial meeting, whether there is anything that could be troubling or depressing within the story of your client. It is essential to be aware because this can influence your choice. According to the old adage"forewarned is prepared.

Make a habit of learning from my mistakes

In our first encounter, Pat handed me an outline of her tale. The story began when she was a young girl who lived in a small town in the Welsh Valleys but she had always wanted to go on. After escaping and experiencing numerous adventures, she came across and was in love with a powerful and wealthy man. The story she told was about their lives together. (Mentioned in the first chapter under the "shock factor.) The story didn't come to a happy ending and she warned me. The story was one of rags-to-riches and a rags-to-riches tale. I enjoyed Pat I liked her, and we're staying in touch, but after she had finished writing her story an agent with a name in the industry came along and persuaded her to share the whole story. A task I'd clearly missed! The next time we met, she seemed withdrawn, and I felt that she was uneasy with some thing. Then she stated "I suppose I should tell you about the paedophilia."

It is best not to be surprised this kind of thing, especially in the midst of your project. Take the bad bits out of your client before deciding.

Make sure your mouth is closed

Moral judgments, political opinions and religion, or any other views about life must remain private when conducting interviews with clients. The ghostwriter, must be able to keep your mouth shut and not reveal your views from being revealed to others.

"I do not agree with what you have to say, but I'll defend to the death your right to say it," are phrases from Voltaire perhaps Oscar Wilde or even Evelyn Hall. These words have been associated with numerous wise men, but regardless of the person who invented them initially They are worth recollecting whenever you're considering the opinions of people that you don't agree with.

Be wary of taking on the project in case you do not agree with the viewpoints of the author. They will likely repeat in the projects they ask to be able to complete or, if you're a brand new writer, it can be difficult to take a take a step back to finish the work for something that completely contradicts your views. If you truly believe that you're able to remain non-judgmental, you can affirm this. Professionals have been taught to not judge.

What are the signs to watch out for?

Certain kinds of clients must be kept out of. If someone seems puzzled, perhaps it could prove to be a huge hassle.

Janie Jackson tells us the story of her attempts to write the autobiography of a former colonel.

The first time we met was kind of getting to know each other conversation, though I believe the Colonel was talking about the ducks before I even got there. Second time, I attempted to establish some sort of order through saying that it'd be better for us all if we began at the beginning, where he was raised, born, etc.--but that immediately set an alarm on ducks. There's a hazy notion that geese were mentioned too. It seems like I can remember in the middle of the fourth meeting, he enthusiastically handed me "some notes that I've prepared to you"-- dreadful scratching on an exercise book-- about ducks! For three months I saw the man six times and did not go beyond how the way he played with ducks on the farm as just a child! I was also not invited to a cup of tea! In hindsight, I realize that I could have insist upon more management. Give him a specific time frame to blog about, say. In the event that some part of the circumstances were clearly because of my lack of experience and I began with the idea of talking to him to allow me to jump into the fascinating bits before obtaining more information.'

Some clients in their lives because they are associated with a particular subject such as mountaineering, medicine or mountaineering, must clearly explain matters or necessitate a significant amount of research.

"I interviewed a former chauffeur of famous steam locomotive Flying Scotsman to write a story for Steam Railway magazine. The interview quickly revealed that the driver had lived an amazing life. I thought about the possibility of ghostwriting his personal story. We would meet weekly for several months. This was kind of like peeling away the onion's layers. There was always something new to learn It was all was fascinating. He was great to work with and made himself accessible regularly, making him a perfect interviewer.

While I was accumulating details and information, I noticed that when he reminisced about certain experiences the man would recall various things at different times. I'd think I'd done my best to cover a subject but then discover after a few months the most important details were absent. In some instances, it was due to my inexperience regarding this particular area. This specific subject area is where precision is crucial and there are many who have more expertise that I. Therefore, I've come to the conclusion that this project isn't the right idea that I can undertake.'

Glynis Scrivens

If they seem unsure of everything. Perhaps they hesitate when you discuss certain aspects of the story. They might make statements like "It might be best if we skipped that bit," or "We'll leave that out, shall we?" It's nothing more frustrating than making the work only to discover that the client later on that they have changed their mind on the whole project. If you think a customer isn't sure if they'd like their work to go through the day, it's best to tell your client a "no thank-you.

"My client made a decision after a few months of the writing project that she would like I stop promoting her novel to agents and publishers. She rethought her decision about making it available to the general public.'

Julia Anderson

This is the story of a good-hearted person who felt that an individual's story could be recorded.

An acquaintance mentioned she had met a person who had stories that needed to be shared. He definitely sounded like an interesting personality. To begin with the man had trained an ape as his assistant in the office. The ape was able to, upon an order, access the safe combination. It could also bring documents. He was also vital. "Tell me more," I asked.

www.ingramcontent.com/pod-product-compliance
Lightning Source LLC
Chambersburg PA
CBHW071441080526
44587CB00014B/1946